D0129490

CHAMPLAIN

Archives of Ontario, F1152, Container 3, Series B293935.

The Champlain monument in Orillia, Ontario. It was unveiled on July 1, 1925, at Couchiching Beach Park. Standing at over nine metres high, the monument was created in England by artist Vernon March and shipped to Canada.

CHAMPLAIN

Peacemaker and Explorer

MARY BEACOCK FRYER

DUNDURN
TORONTO

Copyright © Mary Beacock Fryer, 2011

All rights reserved. No part of this publication may be reproduced, stored in a retrieval system, or transmitted in any form or by any means, electronic, mechanical, photocopying, recording, or otherwise (except for brief passages for purposes of review) without the prior permission of Dundurn Press. Permission to photocopy should be requested from Access Copyright.

Editor: Shannon Whibbs
Design: Courtney Horner
Printer: Webcom

Library and Archives Canada Cataloguing in Publication

Fryer, Mary Beacock, 1929-
      Champlain : peacemaker and explorer / written by
Mary Beacock Fryer.

Includes bibliographical references and index.
Issued also in electronic formats.
ISBN 978-1-55488-940-2

      1. Champlain, Samuel de, 1567-1635--Juvenile
literature. 2. Explorers--France--Biography--Juvenile
literature. 3. Explorers--Canada--Biography--Juvenile
literature. 4. Canada--Discovery and exploration--
French--Juvenile literature. 5. Canada--History--To 1663
(New France)--Juvenile literature. I. Title.

FC332.F79 2011   j971.01'13092   C2011-901915-9

1   2   3   4   5   15   14   13   12   11

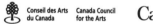

We acknowledge the support of the **Canada Council for the Arts** and the **Ontario Arts Council** for our publishing program. We also acknowledge the financial support of the **Government of Canada** through the **Canada Book Fund** and **Livres Canada Books**, and the **Government of Ontario** through the **Ontario Book Publishing Tax Credit** and the **Ontario Media Development Corporation**.

Care has been taken to trace the ownership of copyright material used in this book. The author and the publisher welcome any information enabling them to rectify any references or credits in subsequent editions.

J. Kirk Howard, President

Printed and bound in Canada.
www.dundurn.com

Dundurn	Gazelle Book Services Limited	Dundurn
3 Church Street, Suite 500	White Cross Mills	2250 Military Road
Toronto, Ontario, Canada	High Town, Lancaster, England	Tonawanda, NY
M5E 1M2	LA1 4XS	U.S.A. 14150

Contents

Acknowledgements

Most important was David Hackett Fischer's 834-page work, *Champlain's Dream* (2008), that brought a valuable new light on the life of this founding father of Canada.

I owe much to the love of my life, Geoffrey R.D. Fryer, always patient, always so supportive. I would not have succeeded without him.

My three children and their spouses guided me through the newer aspects of computer literacy: daughter Barbara and John Vandenbroek (with occasional help of sons Adam and Tim); daughter Elswyth and Andrew Welch, loving aunt and uncle; son Alexander and Claudia Fryer (and sons Caleb and Andrew, both at ease with modern technology).

Others include my editor, Shannon Whibbs of Dundurn; Charmaine Sommerfeldt, Customer Service, Archives of Ontario; and Thomas H.B. Symons, founding president and Vanier professor emeritus of Trent University, and chair of The Ontario Heritage Trust.

Introduction

There have been a great many books written about Samuel de Champlain. The planning and celebration of the four hundredth anniversary of the founding of Quebec sparked a fresh interest in one of the most important personalities of seventeenth-century Canada. Canadian historian W.J. Eccles noted that without Champlain's detailed records, the years (from about 1600 to 1640) would have been blank.

A geographer, navigator, explorer, naval captain, soldier, artist, draftsman, cartographer, chronicler, diplomat, acting governor, he was tolerant of differences and beliefs between peoples. Yet his past is fraught with mystery.

When he first set foot in Tadoussac, at the mouth of the breathtakingly beautiful Saguenay River, he was likely in his early thirties. He wrote that he had lived as a child in the French coastal port of Brouage. His parents appeared to be Antoine and Marie (Le Roy) Champlain. Antoine was a pilot, then a captain, who was on call to the navy of France. That accounts for the navigational skills and seamanship. Archaeologists have recently located the Champlain house at Brouage.

There the lad received an excellent education, practical rather than in the classical sense. The Champlain couple have been considered his parents, but there is no record of birth or baptism. Some writers have assumed that the documents were destroyed in a fire.[1] Some also thought he was born a Protestant since Catholic children were rarely named Samuel.

If we do not know where he came from, we can recognize him as a man of the Renaissance. The fifteenth-century awakening is usually seen as an Italian phenomenon; the time of Leonardo Da Vinci and Leon Battista Alberti, which sparked the Reformation. In France, this new way of thinking came late, possibly owing to the unsettled state of the land. As the number of Protestants increased, so did the vicious opposition of the Catholic majority.

With the rebirth came humanism, a philosophy that placed man at the centre of the universe and suggested that people should seek to embrace all knowledge and to live life to the fullest. Exploration was another sign, the urge to find out about the entire earth, to cross the ocean. They were firm in the belief that the land Columbus had seen, and fishermen who packed their holds with salted and dried fish from rich waters to the west, had found a mere thin obstacle. Any day now, a voyager might return after finding a passage that would lead to the riches of India.

I decided to use mainly modern place names, rather than those of Champlain and his contemporaries, so that a reader may follow him on a modern map. I have also been selective on deciding which of his friends, or foes, I would include. Many of the men who could help, or hinder, Champlain's work were of the French nobility, and had long names. I chose to use full titles just once, and by a short form afterwards. Full names are repeated in the index. I have left out the "de"; it may have been added after his passing.

Some readers may find me too critical of French leadership. However, a long-familiar remark was that the French would rather explore than colonize. Indeed, the people of wealth or influence were divided over the importance of colonies. One of the few who recognized a strong presence as necessary to foil the claims of rival countries was Samuel Champlain.

1 Who Was He?

What rather than *who*, is not difficult to discover. Anyone who could wear so many hats must have had a talented mind to have followed so many leads. His obvious abilities brought him to the notice of men of influence; in France this meant the members of the nobility, and in particular King Henri IV. In terms of *who*, we have no simple response, merely rich speculation.

Meanwhile, M. and Mme Champlain were usually assumed to be Samuel's birth parents. They were of the *bourgeoisie*, middle class, but with no connection to the nobility.

Except for the fighting and occasional occupation of Brouage by warring Catholics and Huguenots, life went on fairly quietly. Samuel continued learning his various skills. He accompanied M. Champlain at sea, and studied drawing, sketching, and writing descriptions of scenes that interested him. He also worked diligently on the writing of clear reports.

FASCINATING FACT
Who Was He?

Most sources call him Samuel de Champlain. "De" was unofficial. He may never have used it while he was alive. In his first book he called himself *Samuel Champlain de (of) Brouage*, his childhood home. Later he was styled "sieur," meaning "seigneur" or "sire" — even more than "de" — came after his passing. When Cardinal Richelieu became first minister, he tried to fire Champlain. The snobbish prince of the church wanted only Catholic noblemen in roles of authority!

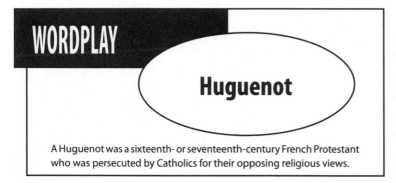

WORDPLAY

Huguenot

A Huguenot was a sixteenth- or seventeenth-century French Protestant who was persecuted by Catholics for their opposing religious views.

Brouage, on the west coast in the old province of Saintonge, was a lively seaport with ships of many nations coming and going. It overlooked vast salt marshes, where brine was evaporated into dry salt. In addition to naval warships and trading vessels, fishermen bound for the Grand Banks called in for the salt they needed to preserve their catches. Many callers did not speak French, and Samuel acquired a smattering of English, Spanish, and Portuguese. Little in Samuel's background explained his later successes. His origin remains obscure. Faced with a lack of evidence, another possibility occurs that involves some observations of the king himself.

King Henri (1553–1610) was known as a fine soldier and strategist in the wars of religion. When not commanding troops or planning campaigns, Henri was a well-known lover of beautiful women. His first marriage[1] at age 18 was arranged and it failed. A second produced the future Louis XIII, and four others. Meanwhile, starting in his teens, Henri was thought to have had 56 or more mistresses, and at least 11 illegitimate children. Furthermore, in the 1570s, he frequently visited his mother, Jeanne d'Albret of Navarre. A strong Calvinist, she was living in the largely Huguenot city of La Rochelle, only 40 kilometres from Brouage. This might explain the anonymity. Babies born out of wedlock to highly placed men were secretly adopted by families of the same status in society as their mothers. Were M. and Mme Champlain Samuel's adoptive parents? This could account for the future neglect of Champlain when Louis first ascended the throne of France. Perhaps Champlain bore a certain resemblance to Louis's father.

When Henri IV inherited the throne in 1589, many Catholics objected to him. He solved the controversy by converting and joining them. He was crowned at Chartres in 1593. He then entered Paris, where Catholics were a strong majority, to begin unifying the country. When questioned about his motives, he was said to have made the famed reply, "Paris is surely worth a mass."[2] Before he converted, the future King Henri had led a Huguenot army against the Holy Catholic League and its Spanish supporters. Samuel Champlain was listed as a billet master in 1593, which would have been just before Henri was crowned.[3]

A seventeenth-century illustration of La Rochelle on the Atlantic coast.

Champlain continued in the service of Henri IV. Nine years passed before the king had control of most of France. Then in 1598, while stationed in Brittany, Champlain received a pension from the king as a reward for loyal service against Spain.[4]

Sometime during the consolidation of France under Henri IV, Champlain followed his example and converted to Catholicism. Life in the Huguenot army reinforces the opinion that he had been born a Protestant.

Brittany was the last French region to be freed. Now the Spanish troops were to be repatriated. Before the king left Brittany on April 13, 1598, he passed the Edict of Nantes. Catholicism would be the established denomination, but Protestants would have their civil rights. For the rest of his life, Samuel would take his Catholicism very seriously.

Like Henri IV, he wanted to see a strong, unified France. Champlain had an uncle named Guillaume Hellaine (or Hallène). Hellaine hailed from Marseilles, and was a well-known navigator nicknamed *le capitaine provençal*.[5] Samuel may have learned part of his navigational skills from this worthy elderly seafarer. The fighting had ended between France and Spain, and Henri was in a hurry to repatriate Spanish soldiers, many of whom were in Brittany. The foreign troops were hated because they preyed on the civilian populace. Among the large vessels the king required was the *(San) or Saint-Julian*, of which Uncle Guillaume owned a share.

With the war over, Champlain found himself unemployed. He began casting about, hoping for a way to go to North America, to see the new world for himself. Then Uncle Guillaume came to the rescue, offering him a berth on the *San-Julian*, soon to sail for Cadiz.[6] This was not the best destination, but it would be an opportunity to travel in parts of Europe that were foreign to him.

As a pensioner he felt duty-bound to inform the king that he had accepted the offer. Henri was pleased that the young man he trusted would be going among the Spanish. He commanded him to keep a diary on the doings in Spain that would be useful. The king was alarmed that the Spanish and Portuguese, as well as the English and the Dutch, were so far ahead of France in laying claim to vast stretches of the New World. The more information he could obtain from the writings of Champlain and other "spies," the better.

When Champlain's tour of duty was eventually over, in 1601, he placed a draft of his report directly in the king's hands. It was not published until 1632, as *Brief Discours*. In that edition is found Champlain's expression that he was "bound to His Majesty's orders, to whom I was under an obligation ... by birth".[7] These words have caused much discussion among scholars, but no general agreement as to what their author meant. Was it an admission that he knew his identity as a relative of the sovereign?

# Voyaging for the King: 1598–1603

The *Saint-Julian*, a "big navire of 500 tons" departed from the port of Blavet (now Port Louis) on the south coast of Brittany, on August 23, 1598. A navire is a large vessel and usually implied a merchant ship. Aboard were many Spanish soldiers and pieces of their artillery. In the fleet were 17 other large transports.[1]

The journey to Cadiz took six weeks. Uncle Guillaume had a house there, where both he and Champlain would stay. Uncle occasionally sailed under the Spanish flag when on charter to that country and he was well-known among the seafaring men. They were anchored in Cadiz Bay for a month, and then they were ordered to cross a wide waterway to the anchorage at Sanlúcar de Barrameda, where the Spanish treasure ships would sail and return heavily loaded with gold and silver, or pearls.

Before the order to move the ship, Champlain had walked around in the main city, noting places of interest to write about in the draft report to the king. Cadiz was strongly fortified, guarding against attacks from the likes of English privateers who also plied the ocean in quest of booty. They were following in the wake of Sir Francis Drake, who had died at sea two years before. Spain was still touchy after Drake's role in the defeat and destruction of the great Armada, by Queen Elizabeth I's Navy in 1588.[2]

Champlain now welcomed the move to the treasure fleet, where he was impressed by the indications of such vast wealth. Here he could glean more information for Henri IV. Meanwhile, Uncle was hoping to find work. When Samuel knew he had plenty of time to investigate more, he travelled to Seville, to do his "reconnoitering," a polite name for spying. He was impressed again by the signs of wealth, like the wall of gleaming gold in a church he visited. He probably reflected on the difference in his homeland, so soon after the eras of civil war and destruction. He liked Spain; he easily overlooked occasions when her rulers interfered in French affairs.

Upon his return, Uncle had some good news. An incoming ship reported an attack on the Spanish-occcupied island of Puerto Rico by a heavily armed and manned English fleet. Rumours spread that an expedition would be sent to that island as reinforcement. Among the vessels assigned was the *Saint-Julian*, with Uncle Guillaume at the helm. At last, Champlain had his chance, as his uncle's aide. Then, to his chagrin, Uncle was ordered to accompany another ship into the Mediterranean. The *Saint-Julian* would be commanded by a Spanish officer.

Again, Uncle was not without resources. He persuaded the Spanish commander to accept the nephew as an unofficial aide. In fact, he may have wanted young Samuel on board to ensure that any misuse of the ship would not go unreported. At last, Samuel would realize a long-awaited dream of voyaging in New Spain, and he resolved to use every opportunity to stay in that large empire as long as possible. Fortunately his Spanish was now fluent, and he would not automatically be taken for a foreigner. That class of person was forbidden by law to be at large in any of the Spanish islands or mainland possessions. He intended to be as capable as Uncle at having his background ignored.

But again he suffered disappointment. The government decided that the regular fleet that carried supplies could deal with the English and cancelled the proposed expedition. However, Uncle helped once more, by arranging for the *Saint-Julian* to join the regular expedition into the Atlantic, and Champlain would be going after all. Early in 1599, the *Saint-Julian* left Sanlúcar for Guadeloupe, and on to the Virgin Islands. From there he transferred to a patache, the *Sandoval*, a tender that served to load and unload the galleons, ship-to-shore, and for exploring along the coasts. The *Sandoval* took him to Margarita Island and on to Puerto Rico, which they found abandoned by the English. There had been little fighting; yellow fever and malaria epidemics had done the work for Spain.[3]

Next, the *Saint-Julian* carried him to the coast of Mexico and Panama. Mexico fascinated Champlain. He was pleased when he was able to return and land at the small island of San Juan de Luz. (He spelled it *San-Jean-de-Luz* after the southern French maritime port.) There he found a naval yard where large vessels could be repaired.

He left the *Sandoval*, accompanied by some officers. They found horses to take them on a short ride to Vera Cruz, and from that coastal settlement they continued along a fine road to Mexico City. For Champlain, the city was the highlight of all his voyaging in New Spain.[4]

FASCINATING FACT
What Is the "Colonial Attitude"?

It is important to remember that the colonial notion of one race or religion being superior to another — while unfortunately still present in aspects of our modern-day society — was the cornerstone of colonial expansion. The very definition of colonialism, according to the *Canadian Oxford Dictionary*, is "The exploitation or subjugation of a people by a larger or wealthier power." The spread of Christianity was seen as an all-important and holy mission. So, Champlain's attitudes toward indigenous peoples is shocking by today's standards, but actually quite progressive at the time, considering the appalling treatment of Native peoples in the New World.

He thought there must be about 15,000 Spanish people on the high plain surrounded by mountain ranges. The indigenous population, living in relative squalor behind the houses of the Spaniards, he estimated at some 100,000. And he was appalled at the condition of these so-called "Indians."

They were converted to Catholicism by force. On Margarita Island he had watched the enslaved locals being forced to dive for oysters that might contain pearls. He sketched several scenes of Spanish cruelty to the natives, and to some black slaves imported from Africa.[5] The Spanish had brought about the deaths of so many natives that they resorted to using the enslaved Africans.

What he saw in the Spanish colonies so sickened him that he formed his own philosophy for nurturing the indigenous people he was certain to encounter in the future. Champlain believed they should be treated as friends, folk whose lives could be enriched by contact with Europeans. The Natives would be their equals, people who should be encouraged to adapt to the "superior" lifestyles, to replace superstition with the beauties of Christianity.

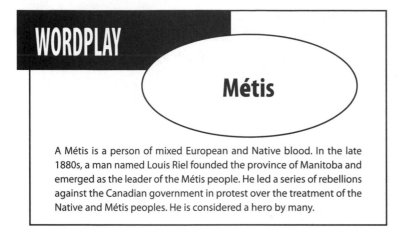

WORDPLAY

Métis

A Métis is a person of mixed European and Native blood. In the late 1880s, a man named Louis Riel founded the province of Manitoba and emerged as the leader of the Métis people. He led a series of rebellions against the Canadian government in protest over the treatment of the Native and Métis peoples. He is considered a hero by many.

Tolerance was necessary in any French colony. Both Catholics and Protestants must be welcomed and taught to live in harmony. Intermarriage should be promoted to create a new kind of people (forecast of the Métis). Champlain was now longing to return home where he could surely find some nobleman to support him in a quest to find a suitable place for a colony in North America. He wanted to be well away from the Spanish, and the Portuguese, who, he feared, might not be much kinder.

However, the voyaging was still far from over. By 1600, sailing again in the *Saint-Julian*, he was visiting Cuba. Next came Cartagena far to the south, then back to Cuba, then perhaps to Florida, but there is a lack of evidence to say for certain. He stayed some four months in Cuba, which brought him to the spring of 1601. Havana, he recorded, was a fine place with a picturesque harbour capable of sheltering many great ships during hurricanes. Now he set off for Cadiz, sailing by way of Bermuda and the Azores, arriving there about mid-August. On the return trip he made no mention of the *Saint-Julian*. The ship had been badly damaged in storms, and was condemned by the authorities in Havana.[6]

Upon landing he went first to see his Uncle Guillaume, Captain Provençal, who was staying with a friend because he was very ill. Samuel moved in with him so that he could take care of his benefactor, and he undertook the difficult task of putting his affairs in order. One item he found was a letter requesting compensation for the loss of the *Saint-Julian* and part of her cargo. By June 26, 1601, Uncle lay obviously dying. He invited his many friends to his bedside and dictated a new will that made Samuel his main heir. A week later he died, leaving his most valuable possession, a large estate near La Rochelle, France, in the hands of Champlain, his beloved nephew. He would now have funds he could apply to his voyages of discovery.

Afterward, while still in Cadiz, Champlain settled down to complete his report for Henri IV while what he had observed was still fresh in his memory. He had tried to write during his travels, but rough weather, and the time spent exploring on land and sea, had filled his days. As his work was confidential, he had also to be discreet.[7] He left Spain in the summer of 1601, arriving in Paris about mid-August. He went directly to the Louvre, the royal palace at that time, where King Henri received him promptly. It was the first draft of a book-length work that would be published in 1632 as *Brief Discours*. The draft for the king was printed in 1601 as *Brief Narrative of the Most Remarkable Things that Samuel Champlain of Brouage Observed in the West Indies.*[8]

Its authorship was later challenged by historians who claimed that the sketches and maps were clearly the work of Champlain, but the text was not written by him. Some suspected that Samuel had acquired his knowledge from old salts on the docks of Cadiz and had written down their tales. Yet everyone believed that the sketches and maps were authentic. This argument had ceased by the time Marcel Trudel's account appeared in the *Dictionary of Canadian Biography*, when he stated that the writing had to be Champlain's. He could not have produced the excellent scenes and maps if he had not observed them personally.[9] The 1601 version might be a fake. Surely the king would not have authorized a printing, because it was not for public knowledge at that time.

The year 1602 was spent partly with his family, or at a shipyard in Dieppe. Most important for Champlain was study in Paris in a basement of the Louvre, where the king employed promising young men to study geography, sciences including botany, or architecture, adding to the knowledge of these and many other subjects. In his role as geographer, Champlain sought to find out why other attempts at founding French colonies had failed. The main cause was poor leadership. Leaders usually went home for the winters, leaving the settlers to fend for themselves. The food supplies left with the settlers were rarely adequate. They had to rely on help from the Native peoples to survive.[10]

At some point before he sailed to North America, he, or others, added the "de" to Champlain's name, an unofficial mark of distinction awarded for a useful service. The other title, *sieur*, implying inheritance, or rank similar to a knighthood, and suggesting nobility, was not likely used during his lifetime.

Facing the fact that he was not of the nobility, Champlain knew he would need the friendship of men who were well-born. He was still a sea captain or a naval captain in his own right. He was able to mingle freely among the courtiers, where he selected two who might support him in his dreams. One was the sieur Aymar de Chaste, the governor of Dieppe, and the other was Pierre Dugua, sieur de Mons. Both nobles wanted to trade with New France and to found strong, fortified colonies in North America. Both were born Protestants who had been given their rights to civil and religious liberty by the Edict of Nantes proclaimed by Henri IV in 1598. Better still, de Mons was a man of the old province of Saintonge, Champlain's home turf. De Mons and Champlain had lived a few kilometres apart, although the exact location of the former's early life is vague.

In command of the ships would be François Gravé, sieur de Pont — ordinarily known as Pont-Gravé. A fine seaman, he had often led transatlantic voyages to trade with the Natives for valuable cargo. While Champlain concentrated on his reports, Pont-Gravé would handle the trading negotiations. De Mons would assist de Chaste, who was elderly. Both noblemen would remain in Paris to keep an eye on matters. Henri IV was known to yield to other men of influence who were constantly begging him for trade monopolies. Trade in furs was the best way to be reimbursed for the cost of long voyages.

As part of his planning, De Chaste had secured funds from merchants of Dieppe, St. Malo, Honfleur and other towns where he was well respected. These supporters would assume a full return on their investment, as well as a substantial profit.

3 The Tabagie, 1603

As Champlain prepared to join the expedition, his first duty as a pensioner was to seek permission from the king to take part in the new venture. At the Louvre, Henri IV eagerly approved. He instructed Chaplain to write the same type of report as he had made of his travels through New Spain, but he was also to add his opinion on suitable places for colonies. He was soon on his way to Honfleur, a busy port convenient to Paris, as it lay at the mouth of the River Seine. There he met Pont-Gravé, a large, boisterous man of 43 summers who hailed from St. Malo. He was also of the nobility, a most acceptable rough diamond. Champlain liked him immediately.

The two ships de Chaste had hired were the medium-sized *Good Renoun* (*Bonne Renommé*) and the smaller *La Françoise*. A third ship, not mentioned by name, would also buy fish from Basques and others. It was sponsored

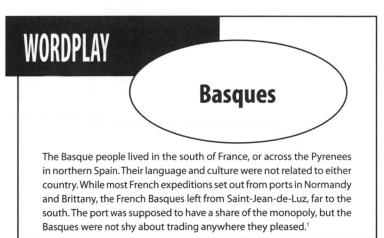

WORDPLAY

Basques

The Basque people lived in the south of France, or across the Pyrenees in northern Spain. Their language and culture were not related to either country. While most French expeditions set out from ports in Normandy and Brittany, the French Basques left from Saint-Jean-de-Luz, far to the south. The port was supposed to have a share of the monopoly, but the Basques were not shy about trading anywhere they pleased.[1]

by the merchants of St. Malo.[2] Pont-Gravé escorted Champlain to where two young men in the latest Paris fashion were waiting. Interestingly, both were of swarthy complexion. They were of the Montagnais Nation, whose land was close to Tadoussac.[3] They had come to France with Pont-Gravé on his last voyage home and had gone to Paris to learn the language and culture of France. The French had wanted to make friends of the Native people.[4] The two, never named in Champlain's account, were to be interpreters. They had been treated like royalty and were thought of as princes in their own country. Their French was excellent, their manner friendly. Champlain knew they would be invaluable as go-betweens. Their language was Algonkian, shared by many nations who spoke its Algonquin dialects.

The ships left Honfleur on March 15, 1603. Aboard *Good Renoun* were small vessels, "barques," which were decked, and "shallops" left open to the weather. Both were oared and carried lateen sails, and would be used to explore in small streams and along shorelines. After a long and partly storm-tossed passage, they moved west, passing to the south of Newfoundland, through the strait between Anticosti, and the coast of Gaspé. Champlain was amazed at the height of the mountains that hovered over the Gulf of St. Lawrence, and at the limitless breadth of the gulf itself. Ten weeks later, they dropped anchor in the wide harbour at Tadoussac. It was May 26, 1603.

From the two interpreters, who had been speaking with some Montagnais they met at the spot, they learned that a festival was about to start at Pointe-aux-Alouettes, on the opposite side of the Saguenay. They unloaded one of the shallops, for Champlain and Pont-Gravé resolved to cross at first light on May 27.

With some crew and the interpreters, and Pont-Gravé at the helm, the shallop soon caught the right breeze. As they sailed they observed huge bark canoes filled with men, women, children, and dogs converging on the sandy shores of Pointe-aux-Alouettes. The shallop was fast, but no match for the swift canoes. In a land without horses and criss-crossed by waterways, the canoe, Champlain reasoned, made the perfect transport.

The festival, the two Montagnais informed them, was the *tabagie*, the tobacco celebration, an oft-used religious rite for the Natives. Several of the Montagnais nations were coming after long days of travel to celebrate the recent defeat of many Iroquois, their

Voyages of "Sieur de Champlain," 1612.

By 2010, Tadoussac showed almost no trace of early French activity. Being developed as a tourist attraction, with golfing, boutiques, whale-watching, and food, it's more like Disney World.

sworn enemies. Champlain was excited that they had happened upon a large gathering, some 1,000 people altogether, a golden opportunity to make a friendly gesture, or possibly a source of useful allies.

The shallop slid onto the beach, and, leaving the crew, the four others began the ascent of what they now saw as the encampment of small bark shelters surrounding a large bark lodge.

The Frenchmen and their interpreters advanced with a show of confidence. Following the interpreters' greeting, some of the Natives invited them to call upon the head chief, the

Sagamore of the Algonquin nations. The important man was entertaining in the main bark lodge. He was called Anadabijou, but whether this was a name or a title, they could not tell.[5]

That dignitary was surrounded, one of the Montagnais explained, by lesser Sagamores, close to 100, who were lighting pipes. They were invited to join the feasting, which proved to be pots of hot moose meat that tasted a lot like beef, according to Champlain's writings. One of the interpreters then addressed the gathering, telling his fellow Montagnais of the kind reception they had received from the French, and what fine friends they were, who wanted to settle in this land they called New France.

Anadabijou agreed that the French could come and live among his people and help them against their enemies. The result, later historians and friends have claimed, was the first Franco-American alliance.[6] Delighted, the two French visitors joined in smoking the peace pipes. They stayed in and around the camp for 10 days. Champlain drew a map of the Pointe and made copious notes. They spent a week going up the Saguenay in quest of better places to settle than at the trading post, but found nothing suitable. The Saguenay flowed far between rocky walls, with poor access to the high ground.

The rest of the time spent exploring (ordinarily Champlain's great love) on his first visit to the St. Lawrence could simply not match the elation he felt over the lucky meeting with the many new friends of the Algonquin nations.

He had only small reservations over how well the friendship would work. During the dancing, young women stripped off all their clothes; young men, too, except for a patch of deer-hide over their genitals. Champlain determined that they must learn modesty. The two French visitors had noticed the cruel plight of captive Iroquois warriors who were stoically accepting slow torture until death gave them release. Victors would need to embrace humane practices. For both objectives — cornerstones of Christianity — Champlain thought that the best teachers would be missionaries and Catholics. Allowing Calvinists to open missions would only lead to great confusion.[7]

They left Tadoussac on June 18, 1603, for the voyage up the great river, following the route used by Jacques Cartier, sailing in one of the barques. Their progress tended to be slow; the prevailing wind was from the southwest and rowing was required to combat the force of the downstream-flowing currents. Champlain liked the level Isle of Orleans, and when he arrived at a vast cataract, he named it Montmorency Falls, in honour of the French admiral, Charles de Montmorency.[8] He was not impressed by "the great rock," *kebec*, the Natives called it, at least not for a settlement. When he was on shore, he examined the soils and found them rich as any in France. They named the delta of the Saint-Maurice River "Three Rivers" (Trois-Rivières), still in use to describe how the river divides into three at the drop to the St. Lawrence. Champlain thought this would be the best spot for an agricultural colony. The farther upstream they moved, the more impressed he was with the quality of the land. He was mapping, sketching, and using his navigational instruments, perhaps dangling an astrolabe to estimate latitude. He was sailing southwest, the reason why the weather was growing warmer.

Finally, the current grew so strong, with many eddies and swirls, that the barque could not force its way upstream. That stretch was close to where the not-yet-named Richelieu River emptied into the St. Lawrence. Champlain and Pont-Gravé changed into a skiff, then to a canoe to reach the east end of the island where in 1534 Jacques Cartier had named its mountain Mont Réal (Montreal). The boiling rapids soon dictated the head of navigation. They would be named Lachine in the days of René-Robert Cavelier sieur de La Salle (1643–1687). As he faced the blocked waterway, Champlain admitted that he had found most of the information he sought. If he tried to find another way southwest they would waste many precious days to trial and error.

It was time to rejoin the *Good Renoun* at Tadoussac. Champlain was well satisfied with his work, from the luck of finding the gathering of Algonquin nations, to the fine site at Three Rivers. Along the way they had met other people who told them of great inland freshwater seas, and of the folk who lived near them. Others spoke of a vast saltwater sea to the northwest. That way might lead to the Pacific Ocean and India and China. The expedition would make a fine profit, and not just from furs, for some of the boats were filling their holds with fish. The sail to Tadoussac was much faster, only a week carried by wind and current. It was now mid-July. Pont-Gravé agreed to spend a month following the Gaspé and Atlantic coasts. Champlain could map and sketch, making the long voyage that much more useful.[9]

— — —

As August was passing quickly, they decided to head for home. From Grand Bank to Le Havre took them only 15 days, a record crossing, favoured by the westerly winds and the Gulf Stream. Sad news awaited them. Aymar de Chaste had died just a month before their return. Both men mourned his passing, while they made good the investments he had inspired. Yet Champlain's work would go on. The trade monopoly had passed to Pierre Dugua, sieur de Mons, the other enthusiastic supporter of exploration and colonies.

De Mons (the surname sometimes spelt de *Monts*) had been appointed a lieutenant-general for New France. He was the first nobleman given such a rank to cross the Atlantic and actually see for himself the territory over which he held awesome responsibility.[10]

Plans were afoot, but in the meantime, Champlain took time to publish his first book, *Of Savages, or Voyage of Samuel Champlain of Brouage, Made to New France in the Year 1603* (*Des Sauvages, ou, Voyage de Samuel Champlain de Brouage, fait en la France nouvelle en l'an mil six cent trois.*)[11]

4 St. Croix, 1604

While Champlain was completing *Of Savages*, de Mons was discussing another expedition to New France, one that he would lead himself. He suggested, instead of returning to the St. Lawrence, and the terrible cold of Tadoussac, they might investigate the lands along the Atlantic coast between the 40th and the 45th parallels. The lands south of the 40th were to be shared by Spain and Portugal, a greatly criticized division because it gave too much power to those empires.

Champlain liked de Mons's recommendation, as long as his friend and mentor could receive a trade monopoly from the king. Samuel also agreed that the part of New France being called Acadia would have a milder winter than the St. Lawrence. They could also search for a more southerly passage to the Pacific that might be shorter. De Mons got his trade monopoly easily enough.

FASCINATING FACT
Champlain's Acadia

Champlain's first year in Acadia was his greatest mistake.

The St. Croix Island site was a prison and a graveyard for the suffering garrison. Scurvy was the scourge! The white settlers had much to learn from the first nations. The latter might starve from winter food shortages. With dried fruit and corn, and with good hunting, they thrived. As time passed, Champlain found that when Natives cared for the sick, they recovered, and he learned much from their methods. In the spring of 1605, the French began a removal to Port Royal, where the hunting was good. The golden year was 1606, when Champlain kept spirits high in the dreary winter by "The Order of Good Cheer."

Acadia failed when de Mons's trading monopoly was revoked, and the settlers were ordered to return "home."

FASCINATING FACT
What Was Expected of the Explorers of New France?

Neither Champlain nor de Mons realized what the government's terms might mean. They did not fully understand the high expectations the French leaders in Paris demanded of men who went to secure a foothold for France in North America. Applicants taking the initiative faced nearly impossible odds. They had to fulfil six conditions:

1. To place settlers on the claimed land to defend a French presence.
2. To explore the new lands and report on their findings.
3. To carry out such expeditions without financial assistance from the government
4. To encourage trade.
5. To convert the indigenous peoples to Christianity, Catholic rather than Protestant.
6. To explore for mines, a source of valuable metals, preferably gold and silver, but copper would be welcome.

De Mons received a monopoly that applied to all of New France, but he still resolved to find out what conditions were like in Acadia. It was more exposed to the Atlantic and more open to visits of fishermen from the Grand Bank, and more vulnerable to actions of the English and the Dutch. Both were searching for a passage to the Pacific. Some voyagers went northeast looking for a route above Russia. In 1597, the Dutch navigator Willem Barents had died after his ship was caught in ice near the sea that bears his name.[1]

Men like the English explorer, Sir Martin Frobisher, pinned their hopes on the northwest. Sir Martin was a vice-admiral under Sir Francis Drake in his 1585 expedition to the West Indies. Frobisher made three voyages, in 1576, 1577, and 1588, to the northeast coast of Canada. He found his way into Hudson Bay, but had no luck going farther west. Frobisher Bay, on the southeast tip of Baffin Island, was named for him. The village at the head of the bay bore his name until the Inuit residents voted to rename their village Iqaluit in 1984.[2]

Champlain may have known Sir Martin, who had commanded a fleet carrying troops sent by Queen Elizabeth I to assist the Protestants in their battle with the French Catholics and their allies. In 1594, Frobisher was mortally wounded fighting a Spanish force on the west coast of France. If Champlain, fighting on the same side, had not met him, he would surely have heard of him or seen him at a distance.[3]

The de Mons expedition, the first successful attempt to start a French settlement in North America, began in 1604. De Mons had asked to be sent as viceroy, or commander, but was refused, although he did fill that role. Champlain thought of himself as a geographer and explorer, but he had no special rank. He was useful also because he believed in the vital importance of collecting fur pelts, and of bringing Christ's message to the heathen nations:

> In the course of time we hoped to pacify them, and to put an end to the wars which they wage against one another, in order that in the future we might derive service from them, and convert them to the Christian faith.[4]

The expedition set sail from Le Havre in March 1604. Seventy-nine men were on two vessels. One was the faithful *Good Renoun* and the other was the smaller *Don de Dieu*. Pont-Gravé was in command of both ships. Some of the men were ordinary labourers, or boys as young as 10, but others were skilled and knew how to build a "habitation" of squared logs. Another nobleman coming to find a place for a settlement was Jean de Biencourt, sieur de Poutrincourt (the latter name for short). Poutrincourt would play an important part in the future of Acadia. Since Catholicism was not yet the official denomination for France, two priests and one minister were aboard.[5]

The ships arrived off Sable Island early in May. From that huge sandbar, they sailed westward across the large open sea until they could follow the coast, while Champlain used the time to map and record. With de Mons, he noted stopping places at LaHave (or Heve); the site of Liverpool, Port Mouton, and at the tip of the peninsula (Nova Scotia), was Cape Sable, a fine location for a trading post. They spent the rest of the summer sailing into St. Mary's Bay, around and about the Bay

FASCINATING FACT
Some Key Factors Operated Against Their Success

1. Trading, especially in furs, and colonizing were incompatible. Clearing land for agriculture meant a reduction in habitat for fur-bearing animals. Consequently, holders of monopolies usually treated the obligation to bring settlers in lightly. They hoped to "get rich quickly," counting on the slowness of travel before an order to revoke a monopoly could be enforced.
2. Lack of interest by French leadership. Men such as the Duc de Sully, King Henri's prime minister, opposed colonization. He saw all the available money as necessary to rebuild France after the wars of religion that had held the country back. Others merely saw little value in colonies.

Metro Toronto Reference Library, John Ross Robertson Collection.

Annapolis Royal, Nova Scotia. Originally founded by the French as Port Royal, this harbour and settlement changed hands many times.

of Fundy and into the vast harbour, which was so majestic that they named it Port Royal. Along the north shore (New Brunswick) they went a short distance up the Saint John River, and on to Passamaquoddy Bay, entering the St. Croix River. Champlain was delighted with the appearance of an island he referred to as St. Croix. It would make a fine defensive site if Europeans arrived, or they found the Native population hostile.[6]

The island is covered with firs, birches, maples and oaks. It is naturally very well situated, with but one place where it is low, for about 40 paces, and that easy to fortify. The shores of the mainland are distant on both sides some 900 to a 1,000 paces, so that vessels could only pass along the river at the mercy of the cannon on the island.[7]

Therefore, he was carrying artillery on the *Good Renoun*. He also had a firearm sometimes incorrectly called a musket, since this was before the flintlock had been devised. His was an *arquebuse à rouet*, or harquebus, a wheel-lock long-barrelled gun. There had been heavy ones that would have required propping, but some were made for hunting, and they were light enough to be fired from the shoulder.[8] The wheel-lock would spin and strike a piece of rough surfaced metal or flint that caused sparks to ignite the powder charge.

The labourers set to work building the habitation, an ambitious project with a fine house for de Mons, barracks for Swiss soldiers, also known as Swiss mercenaries. They were popular for keeping control over labourers or other malcontents and were employed to keep order on land the same way that as marines on ships.

Bunkhouses were for labourers. Gardens, always a top priority for Champlain, were laid out, and buildings were constructed for storage space, in addition to a wall stretching across the low ground.[9] Champlain was a hard taskmaster, expecting all men to work as much as he did. Everyone had to pull his weight, a rule he imposed throughout his time in North America. The site on the island of St. Croix has been called "Champlain's great mistake."

With the approach of autumn, de Mons asked Champlain, who was delighted to comply, to join him to explore farther down the southeast

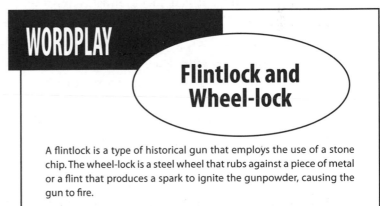

WORDPLAY

Flintlock and Wheel-lock

A flintlock is a type of historical gun that employs the use of a stone chip. The wheel-lock is a steel wheel that rubs against a piece of metal or a flint that produces a spark to ignite the gunpowder, causing the gun to fire.

coast. They sailed in a small boat with 12 sailors and two Native guides, threading their way among many islands and shoals, as far as the mouth of the Penobscot River, now in Maine. There they went ashore to examine the Abenaki Nation's fields, nearly ready for harvesting. They saw the traditional Native way of growing crops — mounded soil with corn stalks, around which vines from beans wound, and squash spread. They resolved to make the same study of the ways of the Mi'kmaq Nation, close to Port Royal. They were satisfied that they had come to Norumbega, the name then used for New England. Now they turned back for St. Croix, as they were running low on food.[10]

Upon their return to St. Croix, Pont-Gravé and Poutrincourt sailed in the *Good Renoun* and *Don de Dieu* to France to spend the winter. De Mons and Champlain were left in command of the little settlement. In October, winter came early, with masses of ice floating down the St. Croix River, blocking the channels on both sides of the island, so that reaching either shore was nearly impossible. They had no source of fresh water with the river so hard-frozen. They resorted to thawing snow to survive.

Food became dreadfully short, and what remained was the wrong kind. There was little to be gleaned on the island. Rabbits had long since vanished. The island was part of the home of the Mi'kmaq Nation, but they were not in evidence because they had no need to be there. Men weakened, and soon were suffering from scurvy without anyone knowing the cause. Their diet was salt meat, and rarely fresh vegetables or fruit that contained vitamin C. Mi'kmaq might have shown them how to survive, but they were wintering in some more hospitable place. Beer, made from fermenting the tender ends of the spruce bush, was an early way of preventing scurvy, as not yet discovered by white settlers. Natives also could preserve berries by drying them, store corn hung up and beans in pits, and they had access to fresh meat through their hunting. As days passed, St. Croix became more of a prison and graveyard than a place of living.

Champlain and his men waited for relief of spring, when the land would come back to life, but the snow persisted until April, and only in May could they draw fish from the river. All told, of the 79 men who had wintered there, 35 died from scurvy, 20 others had suffered but recovered, and 24 had escaped illness, but all survivors were suffering from cold and thirst.[10] Meanwhile, they eagerly watched for the supply ships from France. Champlain had decided that they had to pack up the buildings on St. Croix. The place to relocate was Port Royal.

On June 15, Pont-Gravé arrived with his two ships heavily loaded with supplies and new settlers, but Poutrincourt would not be returning for another year. The next event at St. Croix, with de Mons and Pont-Gravé's approval, was the move to Port Royal. Buildings were taken down to be reassembled at the better site. With that move complete, conditions began to improve.

FASCINATING FACT
The Danger of Scurvy

Scurvy is a disease that is caused by a lack of vitamin C in the human body. This dreadful affliction was common amongst sea-bound explorers because of their poor diet. The symptoms were spots on the skin, and spongy gums, which eventually causes teeth to fall out. Even after the cause of scurvy was discovered, it continued to be a problem because there was no way to store fresh fruits and vegetables without them rotting over the course of a long voyage. In later days, ships started carrying canned fruits and vegetables, but the cans were sealed with lead, so the men often became ill — and sometimes died — from lead poisoning!

5 Port Royal: The First Season, Autumn 1605–Spring 1606

The labour of moving the habitation across the Bay of Fundy was no joke. The survivors of the past winter and the new men worked well into the summer before the task was even half completed. As well, the men had to become acquainted with the surrounding countryside. In most ways it seemed a happy place, well watered by streams, with views of rolling country among the forests. They soon visited their neighbours of the Mi'kmaq Nation, who were friendly and helpful. As at the Kennebec, Champlain saw fields where corn, beans, squash, melons, and tobacco would soon be growing. The soil was rich; the corn would be at least as high as a man by September.

De Mons stayed in command until he thought everything was proceeding well, then he left in haste, eager to be in France, where powerful enemies at court might be working against him. He appointed Pont-Gravé lieutenant of Port Royal. Champlain had the option of going with de Mons or to continue exploring. He decided to stay. With Pont-Gravé he would move into the commandant's fine house and enjoy its luxuries.[1]

Late in March, Pont-Gravé and Champlain set out in a barque from the great harbour to follow the coast of Acadia. They had a disturbing attack from the Fundy tides that threw their boat high upon jutting rocks. The crew and the few passengers aboard escaped with their lives, but the exploration had suffered a setback.

Closer to the habitation they got on well with the Mi'kmaq leaders, and people they called "Souriquois."[2] At their dinners in the newly built habitation, Mi'kmaq, but also men of other nations were present, enjoying the Frenchmen's hospitality. Men mixed happily together. Many writers noted that the English and Dutch never established the warm relations that evolved between the French and the local people. Champlain was determined to ensure good relations above all else.

While the workers were planting and preparing land to be ploughed for grain, de Mons returned from France. He asked Champlain to accompany him on a voyage along the coast of New England. He wanted to see for himself the lands his geographer had visited the autumn before. Much work still had to be supervised, but de Mons was the employer. The noble leader hoped to reach the coast of Florida, but they were stopped after a nasty encounter with some Natives at Cape Cod.[3]

While de Mons and an escort of his men-at-arms were marching along the shore, the soldiers stole some ripe corn. The Natives, friendly at first, now turned dangerous. After one Native had been taken prisoner to a ship, one of de Mons's sailors was killed by arrows and knives. The visitors left in haste and set out for distant Port Royal.[4]

In his own writing, Champlain kept his angry feelings to himself. This was perhaps his main drawback as a reporter. Knowing how strongly he believed in fair play for the indigenous folk, he had to have been furious with de Mons for not controlling his men. Yet he was helpless to interfere or let his emotions surface. Keeping in de Mons's good graces was absolutely necessary if he wanted to continue his life's passion.

During August and early September, what remained of the colony on St. Croix was moved across the Bay of Fundy. De Mons and Poutrincourt now left for the long journey home to France. Pont-Gravé, with Champlain as second in command, would govern the colony until supply ships and new settlers could arrive in the spring.

Before going into quarters for the winter, Champlain made one visit across the Bay of Fundy to the Saint John River Valley, hoping to find someone who could show him a copper-mine site. Despite many tales that Acadia had plenty of mountains where copper supposedly was mined, he admitted that he had failed to find any evidence.

The second winter in Acadia was much more comfortable than on the Island of St. Croix. Still, out of 80 residents, some 12 died from scurvy and five recovered, while a few died of other causes. For the time, that was considered good luck. Isolation was never as severe because transport did not close down as it did at St. Croix; the harbour at Port Royal was salty and did not freeze over, so supply ships were able to pass. They were able to hunt in the country beyond the habitation, although they still depended on regular provisions from home.

A cause of discontent lingered because of the length of the winter, even though snow did not fall until December, later than at St. Croix. Still, the months were dull and boring, with little to improve the outlook of the residents. Champlain knew he must think of a way to lift spirits if the colony was to survive a third bitterly cold season. Toward the end of the winter, the stocks of wine and other provisions were nearly gone.

Low spirits revived with the coming of good weather, but the eagerly anticipated fleet of supply ships failed to appear. In June some settlers left in shallops hoping to reach the Atlantic coast and find a fisherman who would give them a passage home. They were still far from the trading post at Canso — their hope— when a French ship appeared. On board they found de Mons's secretary, who told them that a supply ship had arrived at Canso and would be heading for Port Royal any day.[5]

# 6 Port Royal: The Golden Year, 1606–1607

The wonderfully successful year began in July with the return of Jean de Biencourt, sieur de Poutrincourt, with his son, Charles de Biencourt. They brought some 50 recruits for the colony, and a land grant surrounding Port Royal, where he would establish his own feudal seigneury. Among the recruits were labourers, a few aristocrats, a cousin from Paris, and an apothecary and horticulturalist named Louis Hébert. He was destined to be remembered as the father of all French Canadians.[1]

Among the aristocrats, Poutrincourt brought cousins from Champagne, Claude de Saint Étienne de La Tour and his 14-year-old son, Charles. One day Charles would be a governor of Acadia.

Last, but most important for that moment, was Marc Lescarbot, lawyer, poet, dramatist, and writer of bright narrative. As a recorder, he was the complete opposite of Samuel Champlain. Where the latter wrote in great detail of the things he thought were important, and without much sparkle, the former was a born storyteller whose work was alive with anecdotes. He wrote the first play performed in Canada, *Le Théâtre de Neptune*. It was in a watery setting, taking place in boats along the shore.[2]

En route to Port Royal, when his ship was anchored at Canso, Lescarbot wrote:

Two long-boats came up, one manned with savages, who had a moose painted on their sail, the other by Frenchmen from St. Malo who were fishing off Canso harbour; the savages showed the greater diligence, for they arrived first.

They were the first I had ever seen, and I admired their fine shape and well-formed faces. One of them made his excuses that on account of the inclemency of the weather he had not brought his beautiful beaver robe. He wore only a piece of coarse red frieze, ... with decorations around his neck and wrists, above his elbows and his waist.[3]

At the same time, Champlain redeemed himself by the quality of his drawings, especially of people, which showed details of clothing. Where nearly nude, his details of their physical characteristics were precise.

In September, Poutrincourt, accompanied by Champlain, set out to explore some of the coast for himself. Here was yet another journey to the Kennebec and Cape Cod, in the hope of finding a place suitable for a French colony. As Poutrincourt's barque needed work, rather than delay, he took along a shipwright to make repairs as they went, and carried planks and a shallop. In sixteen days they reached the Saco River (which now flows through the town of Chatham, Cape Cod), where a large number of Natives had assembled, some belonging to nations unfriendly to one another. To Champlain's horror, Poutrincourt was insensitive and his tactics were deplorable. He marched some of his soldier escorts through their encampments with harquebuses on their shoulders, an open threat. They also stole food from the gardens they found.

The Natives hastily decamped, sending women and children into the forest while they removed their bark shelters. Champlain, as with de Mons regarding his foolishness a few months before, wrote of the incident in a matter-of-fact way. His own emotions remained concealed. From the now empty Native campsite, the barque turned north and sailed for Port Royal. Thus ended any attempt by an expedition from Acadia to find a site for a colony to the south. Their efforts were now turned to Port Royal as a crowning success, or to the St. Lawrence.[4]

Owing to the lateness of the arrival of the newcomers, and the distraction of the disastrous voyage to Cape Cod, much had to be done before the coming winter. Poutrincourt and his people were erecting houses, some inside an enlarged stockade. Other buildings would form the heart of his seigneury, away from the habitation. There, Champlain was forming his plan for happier days during the time of isolation from the outside world. He decided that the men would be best occupied by hunting and gathering good things to eat. They could have greater choices than were found in the supplies from France that had been landed at Port Royal. He needed a new order to sustain everyone. He would call it *L'ordre de Bon Temps* — The Order of Good Cheer!

His own account was brief, but Marc Lescarbot had much more fun. After giving due credit to Samuel for proposing the Order, he wrote as it was carried out at Poutrincourt's table:

> To this Order each man of the said table was appointed Chief Steward in his turn, which came round once a fortnight. Now, this person had the duty of taking care that we were all well and honourably provided for. The epicures of Paris on their *Rue aux Ours*, could not have done better provided for, nor at such a low cost … For there was no one who, two days before his turn came, failed to go hunting or fishing, and to bring back some delicacy in addition to our ordinary fare. So well was this carried out that never at breakfast did we lack some savoury meat or flesh of fish, and still less at our midday or evening meals, …

When the food was prepared by the cook, a chief butler had it marched in.

> … napkin over shoulder, wand of office in hand, and around his neck the collar of the Order, which was worth more than four crowns, after him all the Order carrying each a dish. The same was repeated at dessert, though not always with as much pomp.

At night the butler handed over the collar of the Order, with a cup of wine and they drank to each other. They had plenty of game — ducks, bustards*, grey and white geese, partridges, larks, moose, caribou, beaver, otter, bear, rabbits, wild cats, raccoons, and other animals the Natives caught. The Natives were as welcome as they had been the winter before.

> At these proceedings we always had twenty or thirty savages, — men, women, girls and children — who looked on —… Bread was given them gratis, as one would do to the poor. But as for Sagamos [Sagamore] Membertou, and other chiefs who came from time to time, they sat at table eating and drinking like ourselves. And we were glad to see them, while, on the contrary, their absence saddened us.[5]

In the spring of 1607, on orders of Poutrincourt, grain crops were sown, a waterfall, brick oven, and a pine tar oven were completed, the latter for caulking ships.

The time was fast approaching when French women and children could follow their men. Families must be planted. Colonies could never be secure until a population was growing through natural increase.

Everything was going smoothly. The colony was a success. The settlers and their leaders had feared attacks from some of the Native nations, and even more from Europeans. Champlain continued to foster friendships with the first peoples. Most important was the Mi'kmaq, through their chief, Membertou, whose people were the closest neighbours. On May 24, 1607, everything changed. A small barque arrived from France with letters from de Mons.

The settlement at Port Royal was a failure, not through any fault of the leaders or their workers. The failure was at home. Enemies had caught the ear of Henri IV. Traders who slipped in and out of New France had been selling goods —furs in particular — and therefore undercutting de Mons's territory. The king revoked de Mons's trading monopoly in order to pacify those demanding the right to trade as well. De Mons could do nothing to support

---

* Lescarbot may have meant wild turkeys, as bustards were not native to North America.

the colonists; he had lost heavily himself and was in debt to the merchant investors. Another message arrived at Port Royal in July, ordering the settlers and their leaders to return home.[6]

Still they lingered. Poutrincourt wanted to harvest his grain. Others wanted to stay until they could they could bid farewell to Membertou, who was elsewhere, leading a war party. Champlain left Port Royal for Canso on August 11. There he boarded the ship *Jonas*, chartered by de Mons, and reached St. Malo on September 30.

Now his participation in Acadia was over, but his interest in its future remained strong. Acadia would go through difficult phases, but it would survive late into Champlain's lifetime. He never lost his affection for the maritime land. He was proud of his record as the only leader to spend all three winters in Acadia.[7]

— — —

Acadia Afterwards: 1610–1632

First, some of the French-speaking Acadians never left. Second, a new attempt began in 1610, with the return of Poutrincourt, with Claude and Charles de la Tour, Louis Hébert, a Catholic priest, and 20 colonists. In France, a new king reigned. Henri IV had been assassinated, bad news for the would-be explorers. The new king was Henri's eldest son, Louis XIII, a boy of nine years. His mother, Marie de' Medici, a dedicated Catholic princess of Tuscany, was made regent.[8]

Poutrincourt and his party found his habitation intact, and Chief Membertou welcomed them back. The main purpose was profit from the fur trade, and for Poutrincourt himself, a Catholic conversion of the Natives to his faith. A complication soon arose. The commercial investors were Protestant merchants from Dieppe who were intolerant of priests. Then a Jesuit, Father Pierre Biard, sent by Queen Marie, arrived at Port Royal in the spring of 1611. Biard wrote detailed records of his stays — *Relations* — to his superiors. Tension in Dieppe, he wrote, caused the merchants to stop supporting Poutrincourt.[9]

The settlement remained until 1613, when the matter was dealt a blow by an attack from Jamestown, Virginia. The leader of the English force was Samuel Argall (1572–*circa* 1626). He was an admiral of Virginia with orders to expel the French from all territory granted to the English by King James I, who'd reigned since 1603 (as well as James VI of Scotland from 1597–1603).

The council of Virginia further instructed Argall to destroy all French settlements that were south of the 46th parallel. That area included all of Nova Scotia and the south half of Cape Breton Island. He evicted Poutrincourt from his seigneury, burned all the buildings, and Champlain's habitation.[10]

For a time, Charles de La Tour and other Frenchmen lived and were clothed as *les peuples du pays* (the people of the country). La Tour never called the Natives *sauvages* as most writers did, including Champlain and Lescarbot.[11]

La Tour, who felt a true affinity with the Mi'kmaq people, established a new trading post at Cape Sable, on the southeastern tip of Nova Scotia, which was known as Fort Lomerton, after a merchant friend, David Lomerton. The location was safer because of large Mi'kmaq communities in the vicinity. They tended to discourage incursions by English and Dutch visitors.[12]

The first British attempt to establish a colony came in 1621. King James I (and VI of Scotland) granted the lands covered by the Maritimes and Gaspé to Sir William Alexander, who renamed the country "New Scotland," hence Nova Scotia. In 1629, he arrived with 70 Scots colonists and built Fort Charles on the south shore of the Rivière Dauphin. Most of the Scots were sent packing back to Scotland when Acadia was returned to France.[13]

Champlain, then preoccupied with the future of Quebec, was as happy for Acadia as he was for Quebec. Both parts were restored to France in 1632 by the Treaty of Saint-Germain-en-Laye.

7 Paris to Quebec, 1607–1609

At St. Malo, Champlain, Poutrincourt, and Lescarbot disembarked together. During the long voyage, Poutrincourt hatched out five Canada Geese, which he intended as a gift for the king. When he reached Paris, his first duty was to report to Henri IV. The king promptly ordered the birds sent to the gardens at Fontainbleau where, according to Lescarbot, they speedily multiplied into a honking nuisance.[1] This hasn't changed.

Champlain decided not to visit the king until he had seen de Mons, who was living in a pleasant house in the capital. De Mons had recovered from his own disappointment, and was feeling optimistic. The king had been hinting at a new trading monopoly. Perhaps the St. Lawrence River Valley, with its many coasts, would be a safer site than Acadia. Somewhat reassured, Samuel set out for his visit to the Louvre. He must have found the interview painful.

The king spoke affectionately, not aware of the hurt his revocation of the trade monopoly had caused his protégé. He had wrecked a promising French colony, their first truly successful one in North America. The keen explorer did not dare to display his feelings. He would need the king's indulgence again, in time.

Before the close of 1607, de Mons received his trade monopoly. The king's proclamation was dated January 7, 1608. De Mons resolved to stay in Paris, allowing Champlain to be the commander on the other side of the Atlantic. Samuel saw the merit in having his own leader

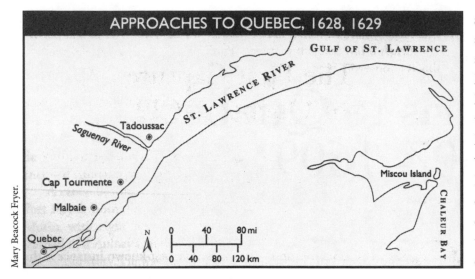

APPROACHES TO QUEBEC, 1628, 1629

Mary Beacock Fryer.

The St. Lawrence River Valley by 1628–29.

staying close to the king and his ministers, as well as grasping merchants looking for favours. He knew he should never again try to remain abroad for as long as three winters. He would need to return to Paris more frequently to defend his interests.[2] While de Mons was busy with the merchants, Champlain concentrated on preparing a "manuscript" map of the coastlines of Acadia and Norumbega (New England). It is still a wonderfully accurate, detailed drawing for as far south as Cape Cod, the part he had seen for himself.[3]

Henri IV gave de Mons his trade monopoly for only one year. On the surface this was not enough time to carry out all the work — trade, sites for settlements, recruiting settlers, converting the Natives, and exploring, not to mention an absence of financial assistance from government. Champlain was not discouraged by the huge task that confronted them. He believed the years in Acadia were a valuable preparation for another attempt at founding a colony. Besides, he now knew how little a trade monopoly could protect the holder's interests.

His explorations, especially along the Atlantic coasts, had revealed long stretches of uninhabited land. A fishing ship or a trader would have little difficulty setting up business in remote spots where Natives could bring their furs unobserved. Many who did not have a monopoly could circumvent the rights of those who did.

He had a new plan for reaching the Native nations in order to learn their languages and customs. Young men, those still in their teens, could pick up new tongues more quickly than older adults, and could adapt more readily to Native modes of life. He recruited a number of lads who were fascinated by tales of the New World and eager to join him.

They came from a lower order in society, boys he could rule over, but who would welcome adventure. He chose four at first, among them a lad named Nicholas Marsolet, and a particular favourite named Étienne Brûlé, a farm boy of 16 whom Champlain found extremely quick and bright.[4] Once the boys learned Native languages, they could serve as interpreters.

He also chose labourers and some skilled craftsmen to guide the construction of his habitation. His workforce was smaller than that at Port Royal; de Mons's funds were also smaller. Samuel inquired about a missionary, but no order wanted to contribute funds. No priest or brother would be accompanying them.

He read through his notes from the 1603 voyage on the St. Lawrence and noted places where he thought a settlement could prosper. The delta at Three Rivers would be productive, but his first thought must be for defence. He was reminded of a narrow place with a high cliff on the north shore that was close enough for a cannon to fire as far as the much lower south side. Kilometres farther south than Tadoussac, the climate should be milder. That would be the best place for a fortified habitation, a spot where by 1601 the Algonquin and some of the Abenaki nations were calling "Quebecq."[5]

As at St. Croix, the more serious threat to a colony's security would come not from the Natives, but from the English and the Dutch, and most of all from Basque fishermen and raiders.

The expedition to New France would have three ships, two for the St. Lawence, and one to revive hopes for Acadia. On the St. Lawrence, Champlain would be in complete command for the first time. With him, in charge of trade, would be his long-standing friend from the expedition of 1603, Pont-Gravé. Of the two ships heading for the St. Lawrence, Pont-Gravé was in command of the smaller one, the *Léuvier*. He set out from Honfeur on April 5, 1608, and on April 13 Champlain followed with a pilot, in the larger *Don de Dieu*, arriving at Tadoussac on June 3.

He found a Basque whaler anchored in the harbour, and learned of a clash between the interlopers and Pont-Gravé. The Basques had been trading for furs illegally with the Natives.

They had defeated the *Léuvier* and severely wounded Pont-Gravé, but they were reluctant to incur the wrath of Henri IV, their overlord. With a second king's ship arriving, although smaller than their whaler, they agreed to pack up and depart.[6] Samuel was annoyed that Pont-Gravé had challenged the more powerful Basques, but relieved that he was expected to recover from his wounds.

Champlain directed his young men to explore around Tadoussac for themselves, and go among as many Natives as they could find. They had good opportunities to meet men of the Algonquin nations like Montagnais, who came to trade, and who stayed in small encampments nearby. They could also be elusive, for they lived by hunting and gathering and did not produce crops. As Champlain had observed in 1603, they were good at packing up and moving on. He wondered whether any Natives lived in villages, and cultivated fields of corn, beans, squash, and melons, like those near Port Royal and along the Atlantic coast. When he had time to think about converting them, the task would be easier if they were not so apt to disappear.

He explored a small part of the Saguenay, and the St. Lawrence, while workmen reassembled at least one of the barques they had brought with them. On June 30, he sailed up the St. Lawrence in barques with his workers and young lads and some supplies, planning to start building at Quebec. The official date for founding the colony was July 3:

> I arrived there on the third of July, when I searched for a place suitable for our settlement, but I could find none more convenient or better than the point of Quebec, so called by the savages, which was covered with nut-trees. I at once employed a portion of our workmen in cutting them down, that we might construct Our habitation there: one I set to sawing boards, another to making a cellar and digging ditches, another I sent to Tadoussac with the barque to get supplies. The first thing we made was the storehouse for keeping under cover our supplies, which was promptly accomplished through the zeal of all, and my attention to the work.[7]

He referred to butternut trees, of durable hardwood.[8] He also had more than one barque with him.

When the storehouse was not quite ready, most of the supplies were being held on barques in the river, guarded by workers. One of them warned a pilot, who informed Champlain that the Basques were plotting to have him killed. The unwelcome guests at Tadoussac had recognized him as an authority, noted the strong control he exercised over his workers and wanted him eliminated. The Basques promised the conspirators great riches. Identified were five of Champlain's workers, the informer, their leader, a locksmith and weapon repairman named Jean Duval who had served at Port Royal, and three followers. The four planned to murder their commander and deliver Quebec to the Basques. Champlain ordered them put in chains and sent to Tadoussac, where they could be more securely confined.

Some weeks later, Pont-Gravé brought the prisoners back to Quebec for their court-martial. Pont-Gravé presided, Champlain at his side, with a captain, a surgeon, a first mate, a second mate, and some sailors in attendance. The informer was acquitted and three were condemned to death, but were later sent to France to be dealt with by de Mons. Champlain wrote that Duval, as ringleader, was "… strangled and hung at Quebec, and his head was put on the end of a pike, to be set in the most conspicuous place on our fort, that he might serve as an example to those who remained …"[9]

The commander and his members of the court were not squeamish about enforcing the criminal laws of France.

All summer the men worked endlessly until Champlain could report the habitation as three-storied buildings, each three fathoms (about two metres) long and three wide, with a gallery on the outside at the second-storey level, and spurs where cannons would be mounted, ditches 4.5 metres wides and two metres deep along the riverbank, and surrounding the whole were some "very good gardens"[10] Actually they must have been very small, for apparently they provided little fresh food. The site was enclosed in a stockade, with gaps for each cannon. On September 18, Pont-Gravé sailed on the *Léuvier* for France and would be back with supplies in the spring.

Library and Archives Canada, C-003164.

Sauvage Iroquois

Though this French illustration is from the eighteenth century, it gives an idea of the appearance of the Iroquois warriors.

Champlain was now in command of 28 men and boys who would remain at Quebec. In preparation for the impending winter, during September and October they joined the Montagnais — whose encampment lay along the St. Charles River — in fishing for eels, which were plentiful at that time of year, but not very appetizing. Some eels were cooked for meals; others were dried for use later.

The winter of 1608–09 was a repeat of the disaster at St. Croix. The first heavy snow fell on November 18. The ice was soon two or three fathoms thick (about four to six metres). Game was less plentiful than at Port Royal, which brought suffering to their neighbours, the Montagnais, who never stored food. They ate all they found on the spot, without regard for the future.

By February, lacking fresh food, scurvy set in and lasted well into April. Of 18 men stricken, seven died; the rest were lucky enough to recover. Thirteen others died of dysentery, or eating eels that were badly cooked or spoiled.[11]

Only eight of the men were left alive, a worse count than at St. Croix. By late May, berries had grown and gave some relief, and on June 5, Pont-Gravé reached Tadoussac with the supplies, and eight men hoping to become settlers. The news arrived by shallop the following day, brought by a young nobleman, a son-in-law of Pont-Gravé.

Champlain sailed to Tadoussac to meet them, and Pont-Gravé gave him a private letter from

De Mons. His viceroy ordered him to return to France, leaving the command to Pont-Gravé.[12] He would obey, but not immediately. He chose to devote the summer of 1609 to explorations, and to his dedication to befriend more Montagnais, the Etchemin nation and other Algonquin, and if possible the Huron people who lived above the rapids that blocked the upper St. Lawrence.

He recalled, soon after he had arrived at Quebec, receiving some Huron visitors from above those rapids, who asked for his protection. He agreed to help, but hoped to achieve, through diplomacy, an end to the fighting between the Iroquois and the others, rather than join in a military alliance.

By the summer of 1609, he was having great success attracting Natives to his habitation. Word was getting around of the French leader's friendship mainly with the Montagnais, but also with other Algonquin speakers. The Natives were looking for an ally against their sworn enemies, the ferocious Five Nations of the Iroquois, especially the Mohawks who dwelt in the Mohawk River Valley.

8 Autumn 1609: Champlain's Harquebus (Arquebus)

Champlain remained bothered by de Mons's order to come home, but he resolved to accomplish some goals before he left Pont-Gravé in command. After much thought about diplomacy, he decided that attempts at negotiating a peace between the Iroquois and his Native friends would fail. The hatred ran too deep. He began to envisage a military solution. For the sake of the fur trade that was bringing France such wealth, he had to stop the surprise raids that made the upper St. Lawrence too dangerous.

He spread the word among the friendly nations that he would become their ally if they wanted him. The response was nearly overwhelming. Warriors travelled by routes that avoided the riskier stretches along the upper St. Lawrence. Allies against the Five Nations of the Iroquois League were Algonquin and Montagnais of the north, the Huron of the west, the Etchemin of the east, and other Algonquin who lived along the Ottawa River. Samuel discussed his plan with Pont-Gravé, who gave his enthusiastic support. Their numbers might be small, but de Mons had sent men skilled in the use of the harquebus, the weapon the Mohawk warriors knew nothing about. What the French lacked in men they could make up with speed and the firearms.[1]

In mid June, he assembled 20 Frenchmen in a shallop, and a large body of Montagnais in their canoes. Fifty kilometres upstream on the south shore was St. Croix. They found a huge war party, 200–300 strong, made up of Huron and Algonquin who had travelled by the safer way, down the Ottawa River. Aboard Champlain's shallop, two chiefs shared the *tabagie* ceremony with him. The waiting warriors asked him to fire his harquebus, which he did, to their great praise, and all agreed to go downstream to Quebec for a celebration before starting an attack. They made a brave sight, the French in their sunlit armour and banners, and the Native warriors, now between 300 and 400, in more than a hundred war canoes. They feasted and danced for a week. Champlain was relieved when the fight against the enemy at last began in earnest. After they reached St. Croix, Pont-Gravé left for Tadoussac to deal with traders, while some of the soldiers returned to guard Quebec. Each day more and more of his allies found excuses for leaving.

By about July 20, his Native warriors were reduced to 60 in 24 canoes. They turned south, up the "river of the Iroquois" (the Richelieu) and found the going hard against a strong current. Fifty kilometres inland, they encountered rapids impassable for the shallop. Champlain considered turning back, but resolved to continue by canoe with three soldiers, two of whom had harquebuses; they intended to cow the opposition. The Iroquois they expected to encounter were Mohawk, the nation closest to their route south, but who were among the most ferocious.

The Five Nations from east to west were: Mohawk, Oneida, Onondaga, Cayuga, and Seneca. Their territory resembled at that time a symbolic lodge, or longhouse. The Mohawks were the keepers of the eastern door. Next were the Oneidas, with the Onondagas in the middle, the keepers of the fire and of the nations' wealth in wampum. Beyond were the Cayugas, while the Senecas were the keepers of the western door. The Mohawk and Seneca were the Big Brothers; the Oneida and Cayuga were the Little Brothers. The Onondaga, in the middle, held the balance of power. Councils of chiefs took place around the Onondaga fire. The league had formed, in the uncertain past, under the direction of two advisers who wanted to end destructive internecine war among the nations. The advisers were Deganawida, who had lived for a time on the Bay of Quinte. The other was Hiawatha (the real one, not Longfellow's), who persuaded them "to unite in peace and friendship."[2]

FASCINATING FACT
Henry Wadsworth Longfellow and Hiawatha

American Romantic poet Henry Wadsworth Longfellow wrote the epic poem *The Song of Hiawatha* in 1855. The Hiawatha described in the poem is a fictional character loosely based the legends of the Ojibwe and other Native peoples and should not be confused with the man called Hiawatha whom Champlain encountered.

By July 29, they finally faced a circular barricade of logs with a Mohawk encampment inside it, both sides shouting in their eagerness to fight. The Frenchmen and their allies explored and paddled their canoes behind a promontory (the future site of Fort Ticonderoga, now a mecca for visitors). There they could remain out of sight of the Mohawk barricade.[3]

At dawn the Native allies led the attack, the three *harquebusiers* out of sight. Suddenly Champlain and the other two showed themselves and from their shoulders discharged their lightweight wheel-lock weapons. The wheel spun, striking a piece of uneven metal that created sparks to ignite the charge. At the time the newly developed musket could only be fired with a lighted fuse and was not practical in hand-to-hand combat.[4]

The harquebus was a mid-fifteenth-century Spanish invention. Champlain may have acquired his during his long sojourn in Spain and its colonies. Of its effect, he wrote, "Two Mohawk chiefs fell dead" and a third warrior was mortally wounded, apparently three men laid low with only one shot. When desperate, soldiers would load more than one ball in their harquebuses, defying the chance that the gun would explode. Champlain claimed he had loaded four, which would account for one firing striking more than one victim. Author Marc Lescarbot wrote that only two balls were loaded.[5]

Champlain thought 1,000 Mohawk warriors had been slain, while only 15 or 16 of his allies had been hit by arrows, which quickly healed. Native armour was made of hardwood strips, bound together with strands of cotton, good protection against arrows, but not firearms.[6]

With the main body of Mohawk warriors put to flight, the allies turned to feasting and looting the abandoned log encampment, and soon began a withdrawal north. When they reached a safe distance from pursuit, the allies turned to traditional vengeance on captives, much to Champlain's dismay. They were repeating their cruelty at Tadoussac in 1603.

The difference between the Frenchmen and the indigenous men and women was cultural. Where Champlain preferred peaceful solutions and humane treatment of captives, the warriors saw courage and bravery as the mettle of a person. One way of keeping spirits up was singing during torture, mournful as the sound might be. Champlain countenanced painful death for a condemned criminal, but he believed in treating prisoners with humanity in accordance with the laws of war.

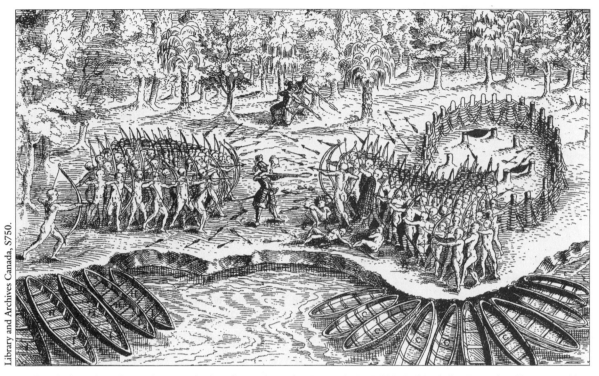

Library and Archives Canada, S750.

A sketch done by Champlain of the battle against the Iroquois in 1609. Behind the French officers are his Huron and Algonquin allies.

The more he saw of Native cruelty, the greater his longing to change their ways became. Meanwhile he forced himself to attend to calculations of some of the distances he had covered.

With his astrolabe he had measured latitude of the battle site as 43 degrees and several minutes. (The latitude of Ticonderoga is 43 degrees, 50 minutes north.) Crown Point, claimed as another possible site, is at 43 degrees, 55 minutes north. This confirms that Ticonderoga was the correct site of the battle. He had also explored southward and found the waterfall whereby Lake George drains north into a beautiful lake, duly named in honour of Champlain.

FASCINATING FACT
What Are the "Laws of War"?

Setting out rules and laws of warfare dates back to Biblical times and has taken many forms over the years, but many of the "rules" have stayed the same over time and these are what Champlain would have been accustomed to. This includes rules against unnecessary torture and suffering of prisoners; avoiding the harm of innocent bystanders; and bringing the war to an end as soon as possible. But these were European rules and the Native peoples of the New World had their own way of doing things, which was a source of confusion for explorers like Champlain, who believed the Old World way was the best way and therefore should be adopted by everyone.

Later in the day, the victors packed up and floated their canoes toward the rapids, and shot or portaged them. The Frenchmen arrived at Quebec on August 1. The Huron and Algonquin warriors from the west had taken the Ottawa River route home. Champlain noticed that the return journey was much faster, flying downstream with the current and wind usually from the southwest.[7]

He next took the time to accept an invitation from the Montagnais of Tadoussac to visit them for the celebrations that turned out to be traditional, with the women stripping, and the scalps shared out. Returning to the habitation, he went to visit his Algonquin friends around Quebec, then prepared to sail for home, in accordance with de Mons's order. He returned to Tadoussac, where he found Pont-Gravé; though he was not fit to remain as governor. Leaving two reliable officers, one a seaman, the other a soldier, in command, on September 5 the two old friends set sail. They arrived at Honfleur on October 10, 1609.[8]

Pont-Gravé went home to St. Malo to recuperate. Champlain rode to Paris, where he learned that the court was residing at the palace in Fontainebleau, and that de Mons was in attendance. He had a most rewarding audience with Henri IV, who was pleased to see him and delighted with his report on the expedition against the Mohawk nation. He presented the king with gifts, a pair of scarlet tanagers, very colourful in their red and black feathers, and a belt of porcupine quills "well woven, according to the fashion of the country, which His Majesty liked very much."

He had an equally satisfactory audience with Sieur de Mons. His doubts over whether de Mons would try to replace him vanished: "I informed him of all that had taken place in the winter and also the new explorations. And I spoke of hope for the future, touching the promises of Natives called Ochatequins [Huron]."

To Champlain they were the good Iroquois. He recognized that their language was Iroquois, kin to the enemy Iroquois to the south.[10]

Both men were anxious to find investors, and they hastened to Rouen, where a meeting went well. They would obtain support for the settlement at Quebec, and more exploration of the country, an alliance with the Huron nation, and a promise to aid them against their enemies. De Mons arranged for one of their investors to look after hiring and provisioning of ships. All agreed that Champlain was the best choice for the command at Quebec.[11]

The two promoters tried in vain to obtain a trade monopoly. While de Mons worked hard, his efforts did not succeed. Free trade was the mood of the day, competition. Champlain concentrated his efforts on what he did best, spreading the word of the great possibilities of wealth through the expansion of New France. His enthusiasm was infectious. Yet he still faced one drawback. He had to work through a member of the nobility. On his own in New France he was the recognized leader of the French, the hero to Aboriginal and white alike against the Iroquois. In France he was hampered by what was perceived as his bourgeois/middle-class origin, his station in life.

9 Second Battle with the Iroquois, 1610

As 1610 began, Champlain was with de Mons in Paris making final preparations for the spring. In February they were in Rouen, and then Honfleur, recruiting artisans and settlers for New France. By March 7, de Mons was back in Paris and Champlain was ready to sail, but he fell ill and the departure had to be postponed. The expedition left on April 8, on a ship identified only as *Loyle*. Pont-Gravé, in better health himself, was at the wheel. The crossing was almost a record; they dropped anchor at Tadoussac on March 26, only 18 days out from Honfleur.[1]

They could see the effect of an absence of a trade monopoly immediately. All around were vessels from many countries participating in a free-for-all; the merchants competing for the attention of the local Montagnais and other nations for their pelts. He was more worried than ever over how de Mons would repay their investors in Rouen. One way was for Champlain to explore, to find places where he might trade before the Natives could reach the other competitors at Tadoussac. Meanwhile, Pont-Gravé would trade, assuming his usual role. First, Champlain wanted to leave for Quebec, to see how his people had fared during the winter of 1609–10. Sailing in a barque, he reached his stronghold on April 28.[2]

He was overjoyed when the officers he had left in charge reported good news. The winter had been unusually mild, with very little illness. He put the artisans to work improving Quebec's defences, and the settlers preparing more gardens.[3]

Soon, a war party of Montagnais came to see him. Their leader warned him that Basques, Normans, and Malouins (of St. Malo) had offered to join them to fight the Iroquois. Should they be trusted?

"No!" he cautioned them. "They say this to get your goods!"

"You speak the truth," the leader agreed. "They are women, who wish only to make war on our beavers."[4]

The Montagnais also relayed rumours that some Iroquois had been seen near Three Rivers. Champlain agreed to help his allies if the Huron would take him to their country, where he wanted to find the copper mines. On June 14, Champlain left Quebec in a shallop with four soldiers who had harquebuses, leaving orders for reinforcements to follow him in barques. They would be French traders, most of whom were handy with firearms. In their own interests they would do their share of the fighting.

Sixty-seven kilometres on, they met a canoe coming from the west paddled by two scouts, one Huron and one Algonquin. They had been heading for the Richelieu (Iroquois) River when they came close to a Mohawk war party of about 100, protected in a circular barricade of logs. It was just inside the mouth of the Richelieu (now in Sorel) but they would soon be joined by 200 more, and another 200 still later. Huge Huron and Algonquin war parties from the west were on their way via the Ottawa River to join in the attack on the Mohawk barricade. It was advised that the Frenchmen should come quickly.

At Three Rivers they found Montagnais from the east waiting, and set off to support the Huron and Algonquin parties, Champlain and his four other harquebusiers riding in a canoe. As they approached the Mohawk position he ordered an attack by the allies, while the harquebusiers would find a clear view through the swampy forest. Weighed down by their helmets, back and breast plates, they were unable to keep up. They were on the south edge of Lac Saint-Pierre, near the confluence of the St. Lawrence, Yamaska, and Richelieu Rivers. Here and there they sank to their knees in the muck, struggling until the attackers could see them and shouted.[5]

The enemy was keeping up a brisk defence, but now the harquebuses were ready. The Mohawks were about to be struck in their circle of logs, piled at least one metre high. What followed was about as fair as shooting fish in a barrel. The experts triple-loaded their weapons and rested them on the barricade, firing until they were low on ammunition. Champlain ordered an assault on the barricade, during which others should cut large tree branches to heave at the defenders. By then the reinforcement of French traders had arrived and joined in the fighting. Some of the braves worked close enough to tie ropes around individual logs. By pulling some of them away they soon managed to breach the barricade and flow into the circle among the Mohawk wounded and dying.

When the fight was over, some 100 Mohawks lay dead, but 15 were captured alive. (The estimates given by the two scouts of 200 coming followed by 200 more to join the barricade had been greatly exaggerated.) Two of the harquebusiers had been wounded, while Champlain himself had been struck through one ear by an arrow that lodged in his neck. Impatient, he dragged it free. After the fighting ended, he had neck and ear attended to in the shallop by a French surgeon.[6]

In the two campaigns of 1609 and 1610, the Mohawk lost as many as 250 warriors. Of a total Iroquois population of between 5,000 and 8,000, this was a shattering loss.[7] The warriors were only about a quarter of each nation of the league. Nearly 20 years would pass before the Iroquois again threatened the St. Lawrence River Valley. By 1630, a strong British force was in control of both Quebec and Acadia. Champlain was an "exile" in his homeland from New France, the land he loved.

In the nineteenth century in particular, historians and others have blamed Champlain's attacks on the Mohawk nation for the years of hostility that came later. Ethnographers agreed that the hostility between the Iroquois, Huron, and Algonquin was of longer duration. Later came a revision, admitting that Champlain had used only minimal force, enough to persuade the Mohawk and their Iroquoian brothers to refrain them from attacking the St. Lawrence River Valley.

Champlain really wanted to end the struggle by a negotiated peace; that was his way. He chose battle to reward the allies on whom he had to depend. That he was successful in warning off the Mohawks is even now not fully understood. Why did he succeed while later men stumbled? His successors, in the observation of American historian David H. Fischer, failed because they used excessive force.[8] This conduct caused tempers to flare and demanded retaliation.

10 Bad News, 1610

Following the two defeats of the Mohawk warriors, Champlain concentrated, first and foremost, on maintaining the friendship of his Native allies. This was a constant preoccupation, and it rested on fragile foundations. Even the slightest misstep could send any one or all his friends on the warpath. He had to be sure that none of his workers upset the Algonquin or Huron, or perhaps most important, the Montagnais, who were so often around the habitation.

He decided to become better acquainted with the western Algonquin, whose land was known as the Petite Nation, and their friends of the Huron Nation who spoke an Iroquoian language. He put together an expedition in barque-sized boats and a few men to trade with the Algonquin and Huron at the island of Montreal (Mount Royal).

With him was his young man, Étienne Brûlé, now about 18 years old and keen to live among these nations. He had learned Montagnais at Tadoussac and Quebec, but he wanted more adventures farther west. Since Brûlé had followed Champlain's orders of 1608 very well, to become acquainted with the culture and languages of the local nations, Champlain agreed to make arrangements for him to continue this work.

When they reached the island (now the heart of Montreal) he found Algonquin from Petite Nation, with a chief, Iroquet, whose people wintered close to the Huron lands. Present was a party of Huron with their chief, Ochasteguin. They agreed that young Brûlé would be welcome in both territories, but they wanted an exchange. In return for their promise of good care, they asked Champlain to take a Huron boy named Savignon with him on his next journey to France. When they had traded, Brûlé went off happily for Petite Nation and Huronia, and Savignon seemed almost as pleased at the prospect of visiting France.[1]

Back home in Quebec, Champlain was worried over so much trading by Europeans. His workers spent their time digging the ditches, putting in a drawbridge, strengthening the palisade, and erecting more gun platforms. They were seeing many more foreign ships on the St. Lawrence. They knew that the English now had a settlement on the coast of Maine, and Virginia was still a formidable threat. In 1609, he knew the English explorer Henry Hudson, in the pay of the Dutch, had sailed up the river that would later bear his name, as far as the site of Albany. The population of Quebec remained too small to withstand any attack, though it was in better shape than ever. More gardens were planted, and he was looking for a site to start a farm. Before winter, Quebec had to be independent of food from France.

In the midst of all this activity, a French ship arrived, bringing word of the assassination of King Henri IV. At first, Champlain was certain he was hearing merely rumours and speculation. For some time he refused to believe any such false tales. But finally he had to face the truth. A letter arrived from de Mons, ordering him to come to France as soon as possible.[2]

He appointed his most trusted officer, Pont-Gravé's son-in-law, to command in his absence. Sixteen of the men of his garrison promised to stay at the habitation for the winter. On August 8, taking young Savignon with him, they sailed for Tadoussac and France. The voyage was a difficult one, taking 50 days before they sighted Honfleur on September 27.[3]

In Paris he immediately learned how the old order had changed. The heir to the throne, Louis XIII, was a nine-year-old , too young to govern. In his stead, his mother Queen Marie (de' Medici from Tuscany) was regent for her son, and she had her own agenda. She favoured greater closeness with Italy and Spain. She was willing to tolerate Huguenots' rights under the Edict of Nantes, but France would remain a Catholic country that required friendship of other Catholics and their rulers. Samuel's employer, born a Huguenot (albeit with a Catholic wife), was no longer received at court.[4]

As he had no power himself, de Mons was planning to leave Paris for the life of a country squire. He asked Samuel to keep in touch. Although he would not have access to the queen regent, his friend would find both admirers and critics among the courtiers. He knew he had his share of detractors, most likely merchants who wanted more access to the furs, or a monopoly on the trade. Champlain resolved to tread gently, but also to work harder. He feared for the future of New France; the colony might be lost because of neglect or quarrels. He was able to seek council from Pierre Jeannin, a friend of high rank, who was known as a patron of geographers.[5]

He had to find a way to improve his standing with the men of power who could be of use. In all of his 40-odd years, he had never given more than a passing thought to having wife or children. He had been too preoccupied with his plans, his many travels, his dedication to advancing the cause of New France. He had not felt close to anyone since the passing of Uncle Guillaume Hellaine, who set him on the way to becoming a wealthy man. Now, with time on his hands, he put together a dossier. Perhaps he could find his way into the aristocracy. Most important, a wife of his choice had to be of the right class. One name drew his attention, Nicolas Boullé, another good friend who held various high ranks in the monarch's court. In 1610 he was minister of finance and secretary of the king's chamber.[6] His son, Eustache, had served with his potential brother-in-law in both Acadia and the St. Lawrence River Valley.

Hélène Boullé was just 12 years old — Champlain was old enough to be her father! She had no choice. Marriages, especially for the real or even near nobility, were a matter for the fathers to decide. Hélène's father and future husband made all the arrangements — a generous dowry from the first, and a promise of her upkeep when he was out of the country from the second. Champlain had worked quickly to make his choice. The contract for this political arrangement was signed on December 27, 1610. The wedding took

FASCINATING FACT
A Political Marriage

Champlain's decision to seek a wife was based on marrying above his own station in life. With the right in-laws, he hoped to be promoted from bourgeois to minor nobility. For a girl, the higher her family's position, the less she had to say about the choice of husband. She could live with her family until she was ready to produce heirs. Since Hélène remained childless, her marriage might have been in name only.

place on December 30, at the church of Saint-Germain l'Auxerrois (which still stands today). Owing to her extreme youth, she would remain with her family for two years before going to live with her new husband, Samuel Champlain.[7]

Among those who would diminish Champlain in the modern day was Canadian writer Pierre Berton, who saw Champlain as a "criminal," an assassin of Natives who was unkind to his child bride.[8] Champlain was thought to have paid little attention to the girl, which may be correct. How many men of 40, with no siblings and probably not accustomed to playing with children, would have known how to entertain her?

He did better by the Huron boy Savignon. He was well received as Champlain's protegé, but Champlain was soon impatient to return to Quebec. Man and boy sailed on March 1, 1611, and again the passage was difficult, full of storms and then fog, and the ship only reached Tadoussac on May 13.[9]

With a crew and Savignon, he left Quebec for Montreal. He found Montagnais Natives, who were starving after a cruel winter, and gave them food. He was anxious to see how Étienne Brûlé had fared, and concerned that snow lingered in patches among the trees. Near Montreal, Savignon agreed to shoot the Lachine Rapids, where Champlain barely escaped with his life.[10]

Two hundred Natives in canoes approached on June 3. Champlain spotted Iroquet and Ochasteguin, and he paddled out to meet them with Savignon. There was Brûlé, lively and in the best of health, clad in a deerskin shirt and leggings, and breechcloth (cotton, obtained through trade). Laughing and talking, in Algonquin and Huron alike, he was very much at ease with his new friends.[11]

Champlain was satisfied. He fondly imagined his young man telling the Natives of the superiority of French life, and of the blessed gospel of Christ. Time would show that he had done quite the reverse.

11 Closer Contact with France, 1611–1615

After leaving the Huron and Algonquin and Brûlé on July 18, 1611, Champlain hastened back to Quebec, where he ordered extensive repairs to the habitation and outbuildings. He took a moment to plant some roses; the place looked too drab! By July 20 he was downstream-bound for Tadoussac, and by August 11 he was sailing for France. He would have to start all over again in promoting the future of New France. The ship dropped anchor on September 10 at La Rochelle.[1]

From La Rochelle he rode on horseback to Saintonge, to confer with Sieur de Mons in his country house. De Mons suggested that Samuel find strong supporters at court, which was usually at Fontainebleau, probably because the new king was a child who would be healthier in the countryside than in the crowded city. From there he set out for Paris, but was injured when his horse fell, and he required some months to recover, losing time he could not spare. By then de Mons was at Fontainebleau, where Champlain went to meet him. Reunited, they met with the president of the council, Pierre Jeannin, who agreed that Champlain must have the right assistance. He recommended Sieur de Beaulieu, the boy-king's chaplain. Weeks, then months passed. Finally in late September of 1612, Beaulieu arranged for him to approach Charles de Bourbon, the comte de Soissons, to ask him to become the governor of New France.[2]

A ship of the period drawn by Champlain on a map of New France, 1612.

After meeting Soissons, Champlain himself agreed that the next viceroy should be a prince of the blood; the high and mighty who could overrule mere merchants![3] The comte de Soissons was the king's cousin. On October 12, Soissons was confirmed as viceroy, and on October 15, Champlain was appointed his lieutenant.[4]

All would have been well had Soissons not died in November. His successor, who was appointed on November 22, 1612, was another royal cousin, Henri de Bourbon, prince de Condé. Viceroy and lieutenant were to get along famously. They had known each other for some time. Hélène's sister, Marguerite, was married to the prince's secretary. Condé offered to help Champlain recruit some Récollet friars as missionaries for New France. On January 9, 1613, Champlain published *The Voyages of the Sieur de Champlain of Saintonge, Captain in Ordinary for the King in the Navy*, covering the period from 1604 to 1612, with a new general map.[5]

Then he planned an expedition of four ships, three from Rouen and one from St. Malo, to carry supplies and settlers to Quebec. He left Honfleur on March 6, made Tadoussac in 54 days, and Quebec by May 7. All was well, and he thought that the flowers were

FASCINATING FACT
Champlain's Ontario

The time Champlain spent becoming familiar with the vast land between the Ottawa Valley and through Huronia has been often neglected in favour of more detail on the founding of Quebec. Yet it was in the heart of Ontario that Champlain was more the man of peace. And unfortunately, it was an ill-conceived plan that got off to a very bad start.

especially lovely. He moved along the St. Lawrence by shallop to the Great Rapid (Lachine) and met with some Algonquin who told him of more trouble with the Iroquois, those from the centre of their lands, most likely Onondagas. He next explored the Ottawa River as far as the rapids at Allumette. He visited Algonquin who lived on Morrison Island, at the head of the rapids, and arranged for some interpreters to meet the Natives.

Somewhere in the Ottawa Valley, he lost his astrolabe. (It was found by a farm boy in 1867 and saved.)[6] Rather than proceed against rapids, he retraced his way and left Tadoussac on August 8 in order to check on any mischievous goings-on at home. He reached St. Malo on September 26, where he planned another trading company of merchants from there, and from Rouen. The result on November 15, was the new company of Rouen merchants, which he called the Compagnie de Condé.[7] Meanwhile, on or about August 13, his wife's parents, the Boullés, had ordered their daughter, Hélène, to take up residence with her husband, now that she was nearly 14. He was expected home within the next few

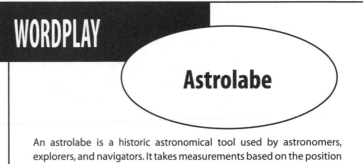

WORDPLAY

Astrolabe

An astrolabe is a historic astronomical tool used by astronomers, explorers, and navigators. It takes measurements based on the position of the sun, moon, planets, and stars, which can be used to tell time and direction. It would have been a very important tool for Champlain in mapping out New France, since this was many centuries before the invention of GPS! Its use dates back to the times of Ancient Greece.

months, and it was high time for her to be a dutiful wife. She was not happy to obey and move in with a stranger she hardly knew — an aging one at that.[8]

On January 4, 1614, Madame Hélène Champlain ran away from her husband's house. No one knew where she had gone, at least no one recorded where. When she was found, her embarrassed parents went to a notary to disinherit her, but a reconciliation of sorts prevented that drastic move.[9] Champlain apparently forgave her and, in keeping with the gentle side of his nature, he tried to be kind. Before he died, Champlain was to admit that Hélène was the only woman he had ever loved.[10]

From January to September 1614, his main preoccupation was securing the commitment of the Récollet order for service among the Native nations of New France. He felt comfortable with the men of this order, which was partly based in Saintonge. The brown-robed Récollets were not a wealthy order like the Jesuits. Less accustomed to luxuries, they would probably be more tolerant of the rough accommodation at Quebec or near the Natives' camps and villages. In Paris, on October 27, Champlain met with bishops and cardinals who were attending the Estates General. They agreed to give him support, and donated 1,500 *livres* of their own funds, about equal to that number of English pounds, a generous sum of money.[11]

As usual, before returning to Quebec, he met with investors in Rouen and found the ships and supplies. He enjoyed the good relations with the prince of Condé, who helped him persuade four Récollets to sail with him. Now the men were looking forward to meeting their future pupils. In November he made a promotional presentation to the court at Fontainebleau, and met the young king for the first time. He found the boy easy to talk to, and was able to delight him with small gifts from Quebec.[12]

On April 24, Champlain and the brown-robes left Honfleur on the *Saint-Étienne*, a large navire of 350 tons, with the still-sturdy Pont-Gravé at the helm, and the blessing of the Récollets. They were three friars, Denis Jamay, Jean d'Olbeau, and Joseph Le Caron, and one lay brother, Pacificus du Plessis.[13]

They reached Tadoussac in a fast 31 days.

12 Visit to Huronia and Lake Onondaga, 1615–1616

Champlain and the Récollets arrived in a barque at Quebec on May 27, where workmen began clearing space for the mission quarters and offices. The Récollets joined in with such enthusiasm that, by June 8, Fathers Denis Jamay and Joseph Le Caron were ready to accompany a group leaving for the trading post at the Great Rapids (Lachine). As word spread that the revered French leader was at the post, the Natives began arriving. They gathered in a meadow at Rivière des Prairies, on the island next to Montreal. After feasting and a *tabagie*, they delivered some bad news to Champlain.

There was more trouble with the Iroquois, not the Mohawks, but with the Onondaga and Oneida nations — nations of the centre of the league. These enemies were raiding the trade routes, interfering with the delivery of Huron and Algonquin furs. They had come asking for Champlain's aid, to do what he had done to the Mohawk warriors, and the sooner the better. They were in a great rush, but Champlain wanted time to plan. He wanted to gather a very large force to strike at the

FASCINATING FACT
Arrival of the Récollets

With his crossing in the spring of 1615, Champlain brought out four brown-robes of their order, three friars, and one lay brother. They would go among the Native allies preaching of the beauties of the Christian faith.

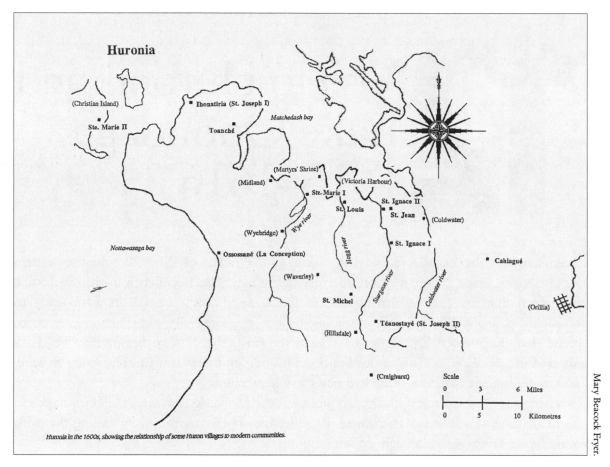

Huronia in the 1600s, showing the relationship of some Huron villages to modern communities.

seat of power of the Iroquois confederacy, the Onondaga heartland. Champlain refused to be hurried; he would return to Quebec to attend to important matters there, and come back as soon as he could. The expedition of Native warriors and French soldiers would need to spend three or four months away on their mission.[1]

They would have to travel by barques on Lake Ontario, then by canoe or on foot. Rather than attempt to live off the country, they would be carrying some food. Hoping that the allies would agree, Champlain set sail with most of his party and Father Jamay. Father Le Caron, eager to start his ministry, had made his own arrangements, to leave for Huronia with a dozen of the Huron warriors The voyage downstream was quick; they reached Quebec on June 26. He was amazed at the progress Father

> ### FASCINATING FACT
> ### Trouble with the Onondaga
> ### and Oneida Iroquois Nations
>
> Champlain explored Huronia and was delighted with this fine country. The attack on the huge Onondaga fortress in the centre of the Iroquois confederacy failed as the allies charged without any organization.
>
> Champlain was wounded and forced to spend the winter in Huronia. Once he regained his strength, he wanted to explore the nations to the west, but the Huron blocked him. Traders themselves, their surplus corn paid for furs brought by hunter-gatherers from north and west. The Huron did not want the French opening inland posts, thereby undercutting their trade.

Jean d'Olbeau and Brother Pacificus du Plessis had made at the mission. The chapel was completed, and mass had been said by Father Jean on Sunday, three days earlier — for the first time ever in Canada, Champlain thought.[2]

By July 4, he was on his way back to the rendezvous at Rivière des Prairies, but when he arrived, the majority of the Natives had decamped. He followed them by canoe with a dozen Native paddlers, some French harquebusiers, and young Étienne Brûlé, along the northern route of 1613, to avoid any hostile war parties. He visited the Algonquin of the Nipissing Nation and by August 1 was crossing into Huronia. He had not been impressed with the rough, rocky terrain typical of the vast Precambrian Shield, but the Huron lands were a delight.

The soil was deep and rich, the style of agriculture similar to the Mi'kmaq country, or villages along rivers of Norumbega (New England) that emptied into the Atlantic. Dwellings were longhouses of elm bark, holding several families, each with its own fire kept in place by a ring of stones below a smoke hole. He viewed the vast mounds of waving ripe corn, beans, and squash, though by September he knew that much of the crop would be harvested and stored in shelters. He also saw huge fields of nothing but corn, and realized that the Huron nation was trading corn for pelts with the hunting Natives to the north. He was overjoyed by what he was finding. The Huron people lived in fairly permanent settlements enclosed by palisades of thick logs, some more than 30 metres high. Conversion of these agricultural people would be much easier than trying to make Christians out of roaming nomads like most Algonquin speakers. The Huron would stay in the same village until the soil was exhausted. Only then would they choose a new site to rebuild their settlement.[3]

He stopped at many villages, to see as much as he could before the warriors would have gathered, ready to travel south in a huge host. On August 17, he reached Cahiagué, the capital of Huronia, a town of about 6,000, on a stream leading to the shore of Lake Simcoe (near Hawkstone), where he conferred with some Huron leaders.[4]

Allthough Champlain thought the population of Huronia might be 30,000, the leaders wanted many more warriors than could be raised among the Huron, and the Algonquin of Petite Nation, near Nipissing and Morrison Island. To the south of the enemy Iroquois dwelt other Iroquoian speakers, the friendly Susquehannock Nation. Called the Andastes, they also feared the Five Nations of the confederacy, and Champlain hoped they might agree to join the attack. On the first of September they dispatched 12 Huron warriors and Étienne Brûlé on a mission to ask these friendly Natives to come to their aid, and to return with a date and a place of rendezvous.[5] Champlain was pleased that Brûlé, always reliable in reporting on places he visited, would be bringing back more valuable information.

The Native army began to move by the last week of August. The vanguard, many small war parties, left to patrol along the way. The main body was on the move on September 1, passing the site of Orillia, along Lake Simcoe, and on by the chain of Kawartha Lakes, the Bay of Quinte, and crossing Lake Ontario close to present-day Kingston, and finally landing at Henderson Harbour in New York State. All along their way they had found deer, bear, and fish plentiful, which made the supplies they carried last longer.

They hid their boats, loaded the canoes with their equipment and provisions, and paddled along the shore of the lake to the foot of the Oswego River, which, despite a strong current, gave access to Oswego Lake, which was shallow and subject to dangerously high waves. They halted on the south side and set up a series of palisaded camps to await the coming of the

Andastes allies. Champlain anxiously watched for the safe return of Brûlé. If they had agreed to come, they should have arrived already because they had a shorter route.[6]

Due south through the woods and fields lay Onondaga Lake, where they intended to surprise their foe. The Onondaga would be sure to have a defensive position somewhere along that lake. On October 9, a Huron war party came upon some Onondaga who were remembered as fishing or harvesting or both — three men, four women, three boys, and one girl. They took them prisoner, and a Huron lesser chief cut off one woman's finger, a signal of intended torture. When the prisoners were brought to Champlain he was furious. He told Chief Iroquet that if women were not protected he would begin to withdraw his Frenchmen immediately. Iroquet agreed to leave the women alone, but he could not promise to spare the men.[7]

On the afternoon of October 10, Champlain and his allies arrived at a large palisaded place, possibly a fort, or the fortified capital of the Onondaga Nation, now thought to be in the city of Syracuse, New York, where artifacts have been found. Many places have been considered, some on the other side of the Finger Lakes. The most probable site would be on Lake Onondaga, toward the south end, between two streams. Lake and stream access would have been the best site. Since Champlain was determined to strike the centre of Iroquois government, a site on any other lake or water front would not have made sense. Champlain later wrote:

> [T]he village was enclosed by four palisades, which were made of great pieces of wood interlaced with each other, with an opening of not more than half a foot between any two palisades. These latter were thirty feet high, with galleries after the manner of a parapet with a front wall of pieces of wood set double and proof against our arquebus shots. They were near a pond that never failed. Gutters were numerous and one was placed between each pair of palisades, to throw out water, which they also had under cover inside in order to extinguish fire.[7]

With the capture of the party of Onondaga, the hope of surprise was lost. Over Champlain's protests, the Huron and Algonquin allies went on a rampage and charged the fortress, but the Onondaga drove them back. The harquebuses of the Frenchmen forced the enemy to retreat. The allies tried lighting fires, but the wind was blowing away from the fort, causing the attackers more discomfort than the inmates.[8]

Champlain had them build a high tower, a European invention, from which they could see what was happening inside the fortress. Arrows flew thick, and he was wounded. One arrow pierced his leg, while a second crippled his knee, and he had to be carried to safety. He did not specify whether the wounds were on the same leg or not. The harquebuses had had some effect, the only means of driving the Onondagas to take cover. After a three-hour struggle, the Huron refused to give up, but agreed to move off for five days to give Brûlé and the Andastes that much time to reach them.

Disappointed when the Andastes did not appear, the Huron finally set out for home. When they had reached the great lake, Champlain begged them to allow him to leave for Quebec with the barques they had hidden there. They refused. The upper St. Lawrence was too dangerous. They fled in better order than in their advance, carrying their wounded in the centre, with guards all around them. Again they found plenty of deer and were well fed. Every other day they erected a triangular enclosure, and drove deer into it. The injured Champlain rode for a while on the back of a Huron warrior, which was painful. Worse, they then put him into a woven basket that jarred him even more.

Once he could hobble, he got lost for three days in the woods in pursuit of a beautiful coloured bird. He had no compass with him, but followed a wide river until he stumbled upon a party of Huron. He was not allowed to go anywhere alone after that![9]

They reached Cahiaqué in December, carrying loads of meat and furs on wooden sledges that they pulled along the frozen streams. In January 1616, Champlain went to the village of Carhagouha, where Father Joseph Le Caron had set up his mission in a small wooden cabin. Together they went to visit the Petun Nation, which lived in the Blue Hills at the southern end of a great freshwater sea (Georgian Bay).[10]

On April 22, they had news of Brûlé when the Huron warriors who had travelled with him to the land of the Andastes returned to Huronia. They had left Brûlé on the trail. He intended to remain to explore that little-known land. On May 20, with Father Le Caron and the French soldiers, Champlain set out for the rapids at Lachine. Below them they encountered Pont-Gravé, who had come looking for them, very worried when he heard from the Natives that his dear friend was dead.

They sailed to Tadoussac, where they learned that King Louis XIII had married while they were in Huronia. At 16 he was of age; his wife was the Infanta Anne of Austria.[11]

On August 3, with Fathers Le Caron and Denis Jamay, Champlain sailed for France, with Pont-Gravé in command, and landed on September 10. The missionaries had returned to urge more help in the conversion of the so-called *sauvages*. He had been absent from France for 17 months — longer than he had intended. The time had come for Champlain and 16-year-old Hélène to try to live in happiness. He decided to name a pretty island near Montreal in her honour. Saint Helen's Island, now much altered by urban development, is still a beautiful spot.

13 1616–1620: Years of Continuing Struggle

The *Saint-Étienne* landed Champlain at Honfleur. He hurried on to Paris, for a reunion at his house with his young wife, Hélène, now a cultured lady of 18. Nothing is known of how her middle-aged husband was welcomed, but there are hints of a pleasant relationship. In Paris, outside, a new viceroy was selected to replace the recently discredited Prince de Condé, who had been arrested for criticizing Marie de Medici, queen regent. The new man was Pons de Lauzières de Cardillac, marquis de Thémines — Thémines for short — a courtier to her Majesty. Thémines, as a *maréchal* (marshal) of France, had arrested Condé in the Louvre and escorted him to the Bastille.[1]

Now Champlain had lost his job as lieutenant to a viceroy. The episode is a fine example of how effective Champlain could be. Thémines recognized his worthy efforts and supported him. By January 1617, he had been reconfirmed as lieutenant in New France. In early March, he again left on the *Saint-Étienne* to make his presence known in June and part of July in Quebec. The highlight of this short visit was the arrival from Paris of his old friend from Acadian days, Louis Hébert, with his wife, Marie Rollet, and their three children. They had come determined to settle, and had been ceded ten *arpents* of land near the present cathedral in Quebec City. They became renowned as the first family to cultivate land in New France, with Marie as the first Frenchwoman to break the soil.[2]

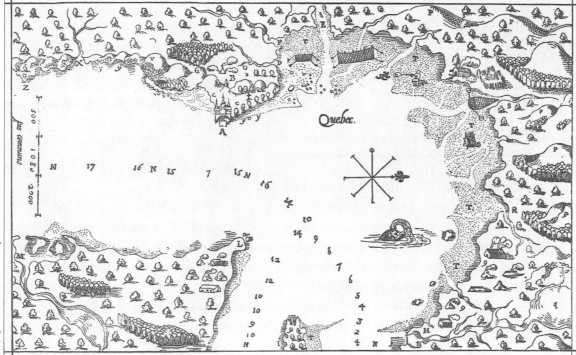

Voyages of "Sieur de Champlain."

Champlain's map of Quebec around 1617.

Champlain also made a hurried journey to Three Rivers to meet with Native allies who had arrived there. With some Huron he found the long-missing Étienne Brûlé, looking, if possible, even more like a "man of the country" than ever. Angrily, Samuel demanded to know why Étienne had failed, two years before, to bring any Andastes warriors to the Onondaga town. Such a reinforcement might have staved off the horrible disaster that befell their Huron allies.

The interpreter explained that he had become lost, and was taken prisoner by some Mohawks. They tortured him until one of the chiefs took pity and ordered him set free. With the help of Seneca guides, he found his way to country he recognized and from there returned to Huronia. He had not come east with the trading canoes in 1617 because he was still recovering from his

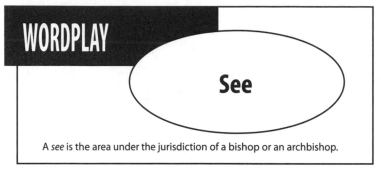

WORDPLAY

See

A *see* is the area under the jurisdiction of a bishop or an archbishop.

wounds. Champlain only half believed him, but could not disprove his story.

He ordered him to return when his Huron friends were ready to leave, and to explore for the great freshwater sea that the Natives had described, and to establish whether it could lead into the long-awaited Northwest Passage to the Pacific.[3] Champlain sailed from Tadoussac on June 14. By July 20 he had returned home.[4]

Two days later, with Hélène, he made a four-year contract with one Richard Terrier for his daughter, Isabelle, to serve as his wife's personal maid.[5] During the rest of the year, Champlain concentrated on a new map, and a carefully worked-out plan for attracting new settlers. Meanwhile, Armand Jean du Plessis, sieur de Richelieu, a young bishop of the see of Luçon, had become secretary of state for war and foreign affairs. He found favour with the queen regent, until a palace revolution against her resulted in Louis XIII, at age 16, deciding to rule directly with his own choice of advisers. He forced his mother to go into exile at Avignon, and Richelieu went with her, but he soon regained the king's favour and returned to court.[6]

Champlain did not find Richelieu easy to get along with. The cleric believed in one established religion for France and New France, and in the stamping out of the Protestant Huguenots in both lands. The lieutenant for Quebec, despite his strong Catholic faith, still saw tolerance as the best way to have peace. Again, he anticipated difficulties with the merchants, his main source of funds, who were nearly all Protestants. When he thought of peace, he meant internal peace for France. Outside, the Thirty Years' War was warming up — German Protestant princes against the Habsburgs of a weak Holy Roman Empire, that was trying to end the division caused by Lutherans breaking off to begin their own church (when this happens, it's called a *schism*). Champlain had loftier concerns, the fostering of everything he had worked for since Quebec's beginning in 1608.

He spent the last weeks of 1617 working on a detailed plan for the strengthening of New France, in particular Quebec and the safe lands along the St. Lawrence. Acadia remained too vulnerable to other colonial powers.

By February 1618, he had prepared two briefs, one for the king, the other for the Chamber of Commerce. Both were to defend plans for the trading colony in the St. Lawrence River Valley. He advocated bringing to Quebec 15 Récollets to staff more missions to the Native nations. Three hundred families would follow the examples of the Héberts, and, for their protection, 300 soldiers. On March 12, the king agreed to his recommendations, but the settlers should not be allowed to interfere with the profits of the fur trade. In other words, he agreed, but he did not truly agree. The same old problem: the persistent conflict between profit and settlement.[7]

Now the time had come for a visit to New France, a shorter one than usual. Champlain was accompanied by new Récollets and his brother-in-law, Eustache Boullé. They left Honfleur on May 24, and reached Quebec on June 27. They rode in a barque to the site of Three Rivers, examining it as the next place for a settlement, and held a *tabagie* with their Algonquin and Huron allies. He was alarmed to learn of quarrels between the French settlers and the Native nations, because of their very different interpretations of the laws. Murder, a crime punishable by death in France, was not treated as seriously by the Natives. He wondered whether the two distinct races could ever meld to create the new people he wanted, again a forecast of the Métis people of more modern times.

They sailed from Tadoussac on July 26, and had reached Honfleur by August 28. As the year end approached, the king granted Champlain a pension of 600 livres. The queen regent had cancelled his earlier pension more than once, only to have it restored by her son.[8]

Next, he moved his household to the fashionable suburb of Saint-Germain-des-Prés, near Saint-Germain, King Louis's favourite palace. The area was popular with courtiers. Champlain intended to use his new location to promote sales of his books, maps, and sketches made from his explorations. His aim, as usual, was to stimulate interest in the future of New France. Here were the high nobles, amateur and professional entertainers gathered to please the king, who participated with them. However, the great fascination was with the

FASCINATING FACT
Champlain and Richelieu

Champlain quietly accepted the Huguenots, as they were better businessmen. Investors in French ports were also nearly all Protestants, unwilling to trust their funds in the face of Richelieu's prejudices.

In Quebec, Champlain acted as governor, using tolerance in the name of peace. He struggled against forces favouring trade over farmers, wealth against food supply, and greed over health.

New France Aboriginal peoples. They were worked into the court ballet, a special favourite of the king. Part of the ballet was the full orchestra, which featured 24 violins. Louis himself was a composer, designer, and dancer.[9]

From the autumn of 1618 to the spring of 1620, Champlain's main achievement was the publication of *Voyages and Discoveries Made in New France, from the Year 1615 to the End of the Year 1618 By the Sieur de Champlain, Captain in Ordinary for the King in the Western Ocean*. It was dedicated to Louis XIII, a deliberate honour.[10]

14 Madame Champlain: First Lady of New France, 1620–1624

To Samuel's great joy, Hélène, "of her own free will," decided that she was ready to join him on his next visit to Quebec.[1] He intended to sail early in the spring of 1619 on one of the ships belonging to the trading company of merchants of Rouen and St. Malo, variously known as Condé's, or Champlain's, Company. Condé, freed and restored as viceroy, was back at court as one of the king's favourites. When Champlain tried to reserve passage for himself and his wife's entourage, the merchants of Rouen and St. Malo refused his request, claiming that he had no proper authority over New France. The king was outraged, and demanded that the Champlain party be given the use of a ship. Louis XIII was the sole ruler, and his authority was not be flouted by mere businessmen.

After many long arguments, sailing was delayed until May 1620. By that time the prince of Condé had lost interest in New France, and had sold his office as viceroy to Henri de Montmorency, duc de Damville and Montmorency, governor of Languedoc, admiral of France. However, he was not to be confused with the admiral for whom Champlain had earlier named Montmorency Falls.[2]

They finally sailed on May 8 aboard the *Saint-Étienne*, their travelling party including Isabelle Terrier as lady in waiting, Champlain's own manservant, and many others, but as yet no children. Also aboard were four more Récollets, and for the first time, an intendant,

Jean-Jacques Dolu. An intendant is a high-ranking administrative, and by 1620 it was an office that was unique to France.[3] The closest term in English might be superintendent. As the lieutenant, Champlain was superior to the intendant, but he resolved to work with him rather than expect him to take orders. Because the ship also carried a small detachment of the king's soldiers, Champlain considered himself, as their commander, the "Lieutenant General of New France."[4] Just before they left, they received a letter from the king, ordering his lieutenant to refrain from exploring and to restrict himself to the good administration of Quebec.[5]

The crossing was very rough. Champlain was worried constantly for Hélène's safety. After seven weeks they were a few kilometres below Tadoussac, where he ordered the ship into a small cove. They anchored there on July 7, to wait until he could patrol for large armed vessels sailing illegally, trading Native furs, just as illegally, for firearms. Competition for lands was growing alarmingly quickly. As yet, news had not penetrated Quebec of the Puritan colony of 1620, brought to Plymouth Rock on the fabled *Mayflower*.[6]

Having satisfied himself that Tadoussac was safe, they landed and continued by barques to Quebec. The arrival was deliberately theatrical to give a strong impression, with fine long-winded addresses so dear to the Native orators; speeches by Champlain; and from the missionaries, masses and prayers.

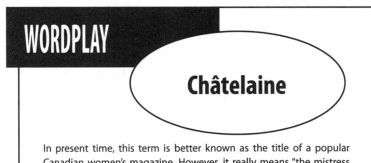

WORDPLAY

Châtelaine

In present time, this term is better known as the title of a popular Canadian women's magazine. However, it really means "the mistress of a large house." As the wife of the governor of New France, Madame Champlain would have had many duties and responsibilities to oversee in running the household.

Little was recorded of how Hélène reacted to finding herself in so relatively primitive a place. She was to stay four long years, endure four Quebec winters. Several sources maintain that she made a graceful adjustment to a habitation now needing to be rebuilt. She was enchanted by the Native women, and eagerly began learning an Algonquin dialect to help her understand their ways. She wore a small mirror on a ribbon round her neck, which intrigued the women. Until then they had only seen their reflections in calm waters.[7]

Was it the dread of another rough and dangerous voyage between New France? One thing is certain: the presence of Madame Champlain and Mademoiselle Terrier led to much new refinement, quieter ways than where all the residents were male! More cultured speech? Fewer naked bodies dashing from rooms or hallways? The whole tone of the place would have been much altered and much cleaner. She was the *châtelaine*, presiding over feasts for special guests. She might have held classes for Montagnais girls to learn needlework and embroidery. She formed a valued friendship with Madame Marie Hébert, who presided over a stone farmhouse. Her daughter, Guillemette, was soon to be married to a farmer, Guillaume Couillard.[8] Hélène needed plenty to occupy her time because her Samuel was so often away travelling in order to meet his many obligations.

As time wore on, she undertook keeping records for him, and doing the equivalent of mountains of paperwork. When she finally returned to France she looked after matters at home while he continued his transatlantic efforts, securing Quebec in the west and promoting it in the east at court or council.

He had arranged for repairs to the habitation, and for the building of a new Fort, St. Louis, to guard the inland side of Quebec. It would stand to the west of the St. Charles River, at the edge of what would become the Lower Town. It would be erected on the south cliff of the *Cap aux Diamants*, "atop Cape Diamond."[9] He still had to travel to meetings with the allies, to keep peace, and to support them against the Iroquois. Actually, the Mohawks had been quiet for a decade since the second encounter with the French in 1610.[10]

He now had a new trade monopoly to trouble him, permitted by the newest viceroy, Montmorency. The old Company of Rouen and St. Malo of 1613–1620, had become the Company

FASCINATING FACT
Chatelaine Hélène

By 1619, Samuel's bride agreed to accompany him to Quebec. Their departure was delayed until 1620, when merchants refused to invest. In May, by order of King Louis XIII, the absolute ruler, the Champlain party sailed. Hélène tolerated four Quebec winters before she asked to be taken "home."

de Caën, under two cousins, Guillaume and Émery. In May 1621, the Royal Council in Paris ordered that the existing, or "old" Company de Caën, and a "new" company would share the costs of a settlement from the profits of an 11-year trade monopoly to found this settlement. The part about founding the settlement came to nothing; the old and new Companies de Caën were not compatible.

In June, at Tadoussac, Pont-Gravé arrived with a ship belonging to the old Company. A faction of the new de Caën Company, commanded by Guillaume, seized the ship. Champlain had to go to Tadoussac, restore order, and have the ship returned to Pont-Gravé.[11] Over and over again, dissent could only be settled by the presence and persuasive powers of a determined Champlain.

Even with the ban on exploration, he had more than enough to keep him busy. Work had begun on a Récollet convent in Quebec; that pleased him, but dissent would not die out and he made laws to deal with it. By 1622, he was encouraging the Montagnais to move close to Quebec, where the land was better than along the rocky Saguenay, and to try farming in the style of the Huron people.

Under the rules conferred by the Royal Council in Paris, the new Company de Caën was settling down, although Champlain was no fonder of its leaders. In June he was sponsoring peace talks with the Iroquois and his Native allies. In July 1623, he met with Huron and Algonquin leaders at Three Rivers, and planned a farm at Cap Tourmente to the east, a road to Fort St. Louis, and next he had workmen hauling timbers for the fort, a storehouse, and for a new habitation. By 1624, he was thinking of going home, no doubt prompted by Hélène, now longing to see family and friends. Only her brother Eustache ever visited.[12]

On August 15, Samuel, Hélène, and their servants left for Tadoussac, and on August 24, they began a voyage to the Gaspé coast where they would meet with three other ships to form a convoy for safety. On October 1, they reached Dieppe. Champlain hurried to Paris to meet with Viceroy Montmorency, the king and Royal Council, to make his report. A new viceroy was waiting in the wings. Montmorency had sold his office to Henri de Lévis, duc de Ventadour, a man dedicated to driving all Huguenots from New France.

Both Champlain and the king wanted tolerance, the upholding of the Edict of Nantes. Also working against them, besides Ventadour, was Armand-Jean du Plessis, now Cardinal Richelieu and the king's first minister.

Richelieu, destined to be his final viceroy, would have a profound effect on the last decade of Champlain's life.

15 Work in France, 1624–1626

Two years passed before Champlain could arrange to return to Quebec. As usual, for a lot of his time in Paris or with merchants of Rouen and St. Malo, he sought sources of money. After the four-year absence, he had to reawaken French interest in developing colonies. His other main concern was more missionaries for New France. The Récollets had become discouraged. The territory was too vast and their finances were hopelessly inadequate. The answer was to approach the Society of Jesus, whose Spanish roots traced to Loyola, an order that had acquired great wealth.[1]

On June 15, 1625, a ship belonging to the Company de Caën landed at Quebec with supplies and trade goods, and the first Jesuits — Fathers Charles Lalemont, Énemond Massé, Jean de Brébeuf, and two lay brothers. All were decked out in the black robes of their order.[2] Their influence would be felt from Hudson Bay to the Gulf of Mexico, from Cape Breton to the western plains "for the glory of God."[3] They had sailed from Dieppe on April 26 after Viceroy Ventadour had compelled the mostly Protestant traders to give them passage. Jesuits were "uncompromising opponents of Calvinism" (meaning they didn't like Protestants at all). In keeping with their greater resources, they were more aggressive than the Récollets.[4]

When the priests and brothers attempted to land, they were stopped by Émery de Caën. Among other pungent phrases he shouted that there was no room for them in the habitation, nor anywhere else in Quebec. Émery, a Catholic who disliked Jesuits, was in temporary command of Quebec during Champlain's absence. At the same time his cousin, Guillaume de Caën, a Protestant, was commanding the company ships in the St. Lawrence River.[5]

The Jesuits were rescued from both de Caëns by a boatload of Récollets and their friends, who rowed them ashore, promised them a home, and half of the buildings and land that they had been granted on the St. Charles River.[6]

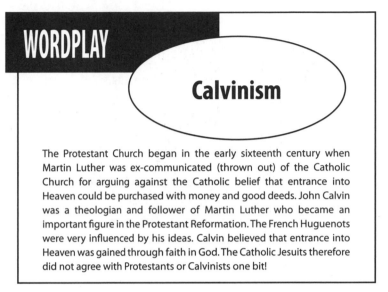

WORDPLAY

Calvinism

The Protestant Church began in the early sixteenth century when Martin Luther was ex-communicated (thrown out) of the Catholic Church for arguing against the Catholic belief that entrance into Heaven could be purchased with money and good deeds. John Calvin was a theologian and follower of Martin Luther who became an important figure in the Protestant Reformation. The French Huguenots were very influenced by his ideas. Calvin believed that entrance into Heaven was gained through faith in God. The Catholic Jesuits therefore did not agree with Protestants or Calvinists one bit!

The newcomers were also disappointed with Quebec. Seventeen years after Champlain had founded the place, the resident population of men, women, and children, numbered scarcely 50. The Récollets joined them in their complaints. The Jesuits found the men of the settlement indolent. The only work they did was gathering pelts and loading or unloading company ships. Otherwise they lay about or went off hunting.[7] Champlain received letters of discontent from both Father Lalemant, and Father Le Caron of the Récollets.

When Champlain learned of the condition of his beloved Quebec, he was unable to do anything right away. He was occupied by breaking in the new viceroy to the duties his position entailed, and with pleasing his wife who had grown distant lately. He purchased a house on the rue Saintonge, a district

FASCINATING FACT
The Jesuits Arrive, 1625

The wealthy Jesuits replaced the Récollets, who were soon withdrawn. A poor reception greeted the aggressive Jesuits and they were not popular with most of the settlers. They were rescued by the Récollets, who rowed them ashore.

more fashionable than Saint-Germain, and closer to her own Boullé family. He sold part of the estate near Rouen, left him by "Uncle Guillaume," probably to pay for the new residence. He needed to become better known by new forces at work. By February, Ventadour had appointed him as lieutenant in New France again. He passed the spring working with the viceroy in his mansion. Respect was mutual, but he did not know what to make of tall and imposing Cardinal Richelieu, whose influence over the 24-year-old Louis XIII was growing at an alarming rate.

Richelieu had been nominated Bishop of Luçon at age 21. After going with Queen Marie into exile, he had been instrumental in a reconciliation between mother and son, and welcomed back at court. He was secretive and close-mouthed. A favourite saying was, "Listen well and speak little" or "Never write a letter, and never destroy one."[8]

Champlain, so very different, wrote in great detail on his voyaging, explorations, and administration, being cautious only to avoid criticisms that would offend persons of influence. He was honest, while the cardinal deliberately used corruption to become one of the wealthiest men in France. He was born of a "mid ranking noble family."[9] Champlain was still not of the nobility. That alone could explain why Richelieu did not want to like or trust him.

The cardinal's antipathy to the Huguenots was soon widely known. He wanted to eliminate them, not just from Quebec, but from the mother country. Across the English Channel, Charles I had ascended the throne of Great Britain in March 1625, and was looking for an excuse to show off his strength. Sympathy for the fellow Protestants might soon provide that opportunity.

The winter of 1625–26 passed. Champlain continued to be busy with Viceroy Ventadour, who arranged a grant of land for the Jesuits close to Quebec. The priests, except for Father Brébeuf, worked at the Recollet convent beside the St. Charles River. Brébeuf travelled with some Montagnais families, nothing that their huts were not very clean. He soon believed that their being constantly on the move made them difficult to convert. While he was in the field the other Jesuits had remained at the Récollet convent beside the St. Charles River.

In March 1626, Viceroy Ventadour granted land to the Jesuits. Word of this happy event reached Tadoussac on June 29, when five ships arrived from Dieppe with more Jesuits, about 50 artisans, provisions, and trade goods. Best of all for everyone, Champlain was aboard the ship *Catherine*, and brought the pleasing news on July 5 for the priests in Quebec. Their land lay along the St. Charles a short distance from Fort St. Louis.[10]

The fathers, lay brothers and artisans began to erect two buildings, one for a storehouse, stable, workshop and bakery; the other as their residence. The last would have four rooms: chapel, refectory with cells for the fathers, kitchen, lodging room for the workmen, a garret as dormitory for the lay brothers, and a full cellar. It was made of planks, with the cracks filled in with mud and roofed with thatch of long grass from a meadow that lay between the building and the shore. Humble though it seemed, they named it *Notre-Dame-des-Anges* (Our Lady of the Angels).[11]

During July and August, Champlain did his best to repair the damages wrought by two years of absence. Fort St. Louis had been allowed to deteriorate and he wanted a start made on the new habitation. He sent workers and some of the Héberts to begin creating a farm on the good soil and meadowland of Cap Tourmente.[12] He planned buildings, and intended to raise cattle with stock from the Hébert farm. By 1627, he hoped to have the colony less dependent on supplies from home.[13]

Jesuit Father Jean de Brébeuf.

He had decided to have the same method of land-holding as in France: the feudal seigneurial system. Land would be granted to nobles, or men of almost that rank if the nobles would not want to leave their already vast holdings. In New France as well as in the old country, the seigneur would rent to tenants who would

Metro Toronto Reference Library, John Ross
Robertson Collection.

Cape (Cap) Tourmente. The cape was the setting for one of the outposts to Quebec. The monochrome grey wash and gouache over pencil was done by Lucius O'Brien in the late 1880s.

work the land and live in humble circumstances. Champlain was no democrat, but he failed to consider that conditions in Canada were different. In crowded France, where most of the land was developed, a tenant would not have a choice. In Canada, he had alternatives. He could become a voyageur, living by paddling the traders' vast freight canoes through the wilderness. Or he could move away from what passed for civilization, live by hunting, growing some food in a clearing, taking a wife with him or choosing a woman "of the country."

From November 21, with the first snow of the season, until April 1627, in the little colony above the St. Lawrence, Champlain endured the harshest winter since his time in Acadia back in 1604. In January 1627, Louis Hébert died in his farmhouse; he would be sadly missed.[14]

With the arrival of the first ships, the folk of the settlement learned that France was on the verge of war. Charles I had done what might have been anticipated; he sent a detachment of regular soldiers to the French Île de Ré to assist an uprising of Huguenots against the stern measures of Cardinal Richelieu. French royal troops had besieged the Huguenots in La Rochelle, and destroyed the English expeditionary force on the island. War was in the wind.[15]

16 The Richelieu Take-over, 1627–1628

By October 1626, Cardinal Richelieu had taken command of the commerce, colonies, and marine matters. In the spring, when the people of Quebec were slowly recovering from the bitter weather, Ventadour ceased to be viceroy, and Richelieu stepped in, taking on even more responsibility. He cancelled the trade monopoly held by the Company de Caën, took personal control of New France, and launched a new venture. It was known as the Company of the Hundred Associates (*Compagnie des Cent-Associés*), or merely the Company of New France. Though the foundation started in April 1627, it did not receive a royal charter until May 1628.[1]

The purpose of the Hundred Associates was twofold: to "market Canadian furs, and to undertake to colonize New France.[2] Richelieu had acted on the advice of another of Champlain's oldest friends, a naval commander named Isaac de Razilly, who was also a distant cousin of the cardinal. Razilly was a large man, but ugly because of an accident in the naval battle off Ile de Ré where an exploding ship scarred his face and left him blind in one eye. He recommended a rapid populating of New France by forming a large trading company to catch up with the populations of the English and Dutch colonies in North America. Incidently, the Dutch had just purchased the island of Manhattan for 60 guilders (24 dollars).[3]

FASCINATING FACT
Viceroy Richelieu

By 1626, the cardinal had usurped Viceroy Vendatour and taken command. He set up a new trading company.

When Richelieu dispatched four ships carrying 400 settlers and supplies, but no armament, Britain's Charles I had just declared war on France, but Richelieu dismissed the thought that the ships might be attacked. The fleet was fired upon by the privateering David Kirke and his brothers, who chased most away. Ships that were not damaged sailed for France.

David sent his brother, Lewis, with an order for Champlain to surrender. Samuel bluffed, swearing that he had plenty of ammunition and food. The Kirkes sailed downstream. At Quebec the French were worse off than ever.

The first signature of the Hundred was Richelieu's; Champlain was the fifty-second signer.[4] Each investor had to pay 3,000 *livres*. (A *livre* at that time was worth about one British pound.) Hélène, in Paris while he was in Quebec, arranged for her husband's payment.[5] Champlain was not pleased with a provision of Richelieu's charter that forbade Huguenots moving to New France. The colony would need more of these competent businessmen as traders and managers of most enterprises. While he was actually ruling Quebec, although not with Richelieu's blessing, he would turn a blind eye and continue his tolerant acceptance of both factions.

In England, Charles I, at war with France since the declaration of March 1627, was plotting a blow against the French colonies. With the king's approval, British merchants had formed their own Company of Merchant Adventurers in Canada, a challenge to the French Company of the Hundred. Charles needed some very special villains to undertake the capture of New France, including Acadia. He easily obtained the services of Jarvis, or Gervase, Kirke, and some of his five sons — David, the eldest, Lewis (Louis), Thomas, John, and James. The surname suggested Scots origin, though Gervase had been born in England. The mother of the five sons was a Huguenot of Dieppe, where all of the children were born. All were considered French citizens, which made their actions the more remiss. Their most-used home was in Dieppe, on rue Écossais, known for its shady Scots operations. Willing to work for whoever paid best, they bargained for a letter of marque from King Charles to operate as privateers, a name almost too civilized for men who would murder anyone who got between them and their intended booty

Some writers have taken at face value certain polite (ironic) phrases in letters that passed between the Kirkes and Champlain. Samuel did not. He could read the underlying menace of these buccaneers.[6]

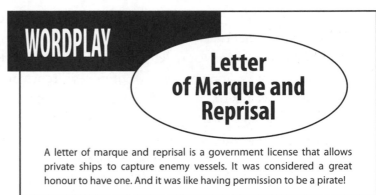

WORDPLAY

Letter of Marque and Reprisal

A letter of marque and reprisal is a government license that allows private ships to capture enemy vessels. It was considered a great honour to have one. And it was like having permission to be a pirate!

In April 1628, Richelieu's One Hundred Associates sent four ships, carrying 400 young men of Normandy, and provisions for Quebec, departed from Dieppe. Someone suggested a convoy as protection in case of attack in the channel, but Richelieu did not think this was necessary. Nor did he want the ships armed. He overlooked any Huguenot captains, naval or private, and chose Admiral Claude R. de Brison, a man of very limited experience in the western Atlantic, but who was a good Catholic (all that was required).[7]

Richelieu's ships were already too late. David was in command of the Kirkes' flagship, with Lewis following, while a third, not commanded by a Kirke, brought up the rear. They sailed to a trading post on Miscou Island in Chaleur Bay, which was probably deserted, and put it to the torch. Nearing Tadoussac, they captured a Basque ship, then a company supply ship under Émery de Caën running ahead of the main French fleet. At Cap Tourmente, they destroyed the new farm, burned the crops, and stole the cattle. Champlain heard that on July 9, the French had reached Tadoussac. There, David Kirke ordered Lewis, using a barque from their fleet, to take a message to Champlain at Quebec, an order for him to surrender the little town or be blown to pieces very soon.[7]

Meanwhile, Champlain had been busy ordering the renovation and repair of the buildings, and Fort St. Louis. He mediated between the French and their Algonquin neighbours, easing tensions between the Native nations to avoid open hostilities, and at *tabagies* he argued for efforts to make peace with the Iroquois. By June he was watching for the arrival of his supply ships bringing the new settlers and workmen.

Back in February, with Hélène away and no prospect of children, he decided to become a father in the only way left to him, by adoption. He would pursue a policy he had long wanted, for creating a new race of mixed French and Aboriginal blood. He chose from the Montagnais nation because he thought them among the finest looking, and girls, rather than boys. Marriages would work better between Frenchmen and Native women. Girls would more easily acquire French graces.

He selected three from among his Montagnais friends, ages 11, 12, and 15, and he named them Foi (Faith), Espérance (Hope), and Charité (Charity). He would take them to France and give them the best education and religious training, to make them suitable for marriages with Frenchmen who would be respectable, but not necessarily noble. He claimed that all were very happy living with him.[9]

On July 10, Lewis Kirke's barque was near Quebec. He freed a Basque prisoner to carry David's letter to Champlain. The acting governor had no intention of giving in without a fight. Ignoring the reality that his food supplies and ammunition were dangerously low, and with the English at Tadoussac, his supply ships might not reach them at all. He lied that he was in excellent shape to survive a long siege. When Lewis reported Champlain's belligerence, David Kirke hesitated. If Champlain spoke the truth, the Kirkes would be farther ahead if they could interfere with the French supply fleet.

They sailed downstream, found the fleet at a distance, and proceeded to block the St. Lawrence to the unarmed French that Richelieu had sent so unprepared. The result was a disaster; most of the ships were captured and looted, while a few small ones turned back for France.[10]

One historian suggested that the Kirkes deliberately destroyed the farm to starve Quebec into surrendering.[11] More likely they rashly destroyed the farm at Cap Tourmente and the trading post in Acadia on the spur of the moment. They did not appear to be men who planned far ahead of their actions.

While the attempt on Quebec was a temporary failure, and they had not even tried to take Charles de La Tour's trading post on Cape Sable Island, the Kirkes had captured a fortune in booty. The loss to the Hundred Associates due to Richelieu's incompetence, was a staggering 164,760 *livres*. The Hundred Associates had been forced to to borrow money in order to put together the required funds, and were left heavily in debt.[12] For the Kirkes, 1629 was another time. They would return.

17 New France Lost, 1629

The start of the third hard winter Samuel had endured was hardly welcome, even though the Kirkes had departed. The storehouse at the habitation was almost bare, their diet reduced to dried beans, some dried corn, and hundreds of eels that the men learned to spear where they had no line. These were scarcely palatable. Fortunately, the Native nations were better off than during the winter of 1627–28, and Champlain was able to send his habitants as far off as Huronia, where the harvest had been fair, and to the Montagnais, Etchemins, and others, where they shared the Native fare. No one suffered from scurvy; the Natives knew how to keep healthy. Of the 55 or so French, the Jesuits had a garden, and families had seeded small field patches while others took to hunting and gathering away from Quebec itself. Still, it was a season of great hunger.

By March, everyone watched the river, praying for French ships to arrive. None did. The Hundred Associates had sent a relief ship with Émery de Caën aboard, but Thomas and Lewis Kirke forced it to turn back. Unable to reach Quebec, the rest of the relief fleet, near Cape Breton, attacked the small number of Scots of Fort Rosmar and forced them to evacuate their fledgling settlement. The French built a new fort close by, left 40 men as a garrison, and sailed home.[1]

Unknown at Quebec, or to the Kirkes, who were moving in for their second attack, Britain and France had signed the Treaty of Susa, dated April 24, 1629, which ended hostilities.[2]

Library and Archives Canada, C4816.

Taking of Quebec in 1629 by the Kirkes. This imaginative representation was published in 1689.

The inevitable seizure of New France would be an illegal act of war. De Caën had informed Thomas Kirke of the treaty, but it was too late to stop their attack. They probably suspected de Caën might be bluffing.

On June 25, the Kirkes arrived in the lower St. Lawrence and on July 20, Champlain had no choice but to surrender. On July 24, now a prisoner, he had been taken to Tadoussac. He later wrote that his people had been treated humanely, and that some had decided to remain. He planned to take his three adopted daughters with him to France, but David Kirke, the professed admiral, refused to allow that. Possibly he suspected Samuel of ulterior motives similar to his own. At 15 or even younger, girls were old enough to become wives, or mistresses. Champlain tried to ply Kirke with fur, hopeless when the Kirkes had already stolen every pelt in the colony.

Daughter Faith returned to her own people. The late Louis Hébert's son-in-law, Guillaume Couillard, escorted Hope and Charity to his mother-in-law, Louis's widow, Marie. Now

FASCINATING FACT
Surrender

In July, 1629, out of food and ammunition, Champlain surrendered to the Kirkes. Neither the attackers nor the defenders knew that Britain had signed a peace treaty with France. The seizure of Quebec had been an act of war. Escorted to Tadoussac en route for home, Samuel spotted Étienne Brûlé, who had offered his services to the Kirkes, certain that New France was lost forever.

remarried to Guillaume Hubou, they resided in the stone farmhouse, and they planned to stay at Quebec. She took the girls in; later they must also have returned to their people.[3]

Looking around him, Champlain discovered that four Frenchmen had deserted his service and joined the enemy. One was a dishonest rogue dismissed as a clerk from the Company de Caën; one a wagoner — and two were his young men! Nicolas Marsolet was not much of a loss, but the last had been his pride and joy as the enthusiastic teenager of 1608 — Étienne Brûlé. Champlain had seen almost nothing of Brûlé in recent years, and had received complaints from missionaries in Huronia about his conduct. In fact, rather than setting a fine example as a French-speaking Catholic, he had "gone native," and become an agnostic, adapting himself to the immoral ways of the young Huron lads toward their women friends.[4]

Many authors made reference to Brûlé the "traitor," but are not unanimous over how he changed sides. First, J.H. Cranston believed that the four defectors had paddled down the St. Lawrence. Champlain ordered Brûlé to go to Tadoussac, where Richelieu's fleet would wait until he arrived to serve as pilot. He would conduct the many French ships laden with supplies and the new settlers safely to Quebec. That would have been in 1628 when the interpreters first found only British vessels in the harbour. Brûlé might have been pragmatic. New France's days were numbered.[5] If he was to survive, he saw the necessity of serving the new strongmen.

In his account, D.H. Fischer found evidence that Brûlé had sailed to France in 1622, and again in 1626, when he married a French woman. On the way back, with a Huron companion (no mention of a wife), he was captured by the British and met the Kirkes in London. Informed of Brûlé's vast knowledge of New France, they coerced him into promising to join them for their intended attack in 1628. When Champlain gave both interpreters a long tongue-lashing, in his own defence, Brûlé claimed he had been threatened with death. Brûlé deserves to be remembered more as an unfortunate victim than as disloyal.

Whatever happened, the interpreter, now aged 20 or 21, was convinced that Quebec was destined to remain a British colony. He had seen the worst side of the brothers from Dieppe, men as much French as British. Cold-blooded murder would benefit no one. On September 14, Champlain, the Jesuits, and other prisoners of the Kirkes set off on the voyage to England and repatriation.

They arrived in Dover on October 27. On the 29th, Champlain refused repatriation, and went instead to London. He called on the French ambassador, the marquis de Châteauneuf, who agreed to speak with King Charles. Because the seizure was in peacetime, Quebec and Acadia should be returned to France. The king agreed, but he admitted he had only declared war to force Louis XIII to pay part of the dowry promised to his sister, Queen Henrietta Maria, at the time of their marriage.[7]

By November 30, as a formality, Champlain had asked the ambassador for permission to depart. When the diplomat gave his consent, Samuel Champlain sailed for France. He would have many loyal supporters, notably the Jesuits, who were determined to return to their missions; courtiers like Isaac de Razzily and from across the Atlantic; and traders like Charles de La Tour at Cape Sable. (Cardinal Richelieu would not be one of them.)

And Champlain would begin years of frustrating appeals for the return of New France to its original owners.[8]

18 Stalemate, 1630–1633

Champlain made his first appeal to the king, Richelieu, and the One Hundred Associates that December, to persuade them to demand the return of New France, reminding them of the illegality of the Kirkes' occupation. Spring brought more appeals and complaints to the French leaders. By April, the king was ready to take the initiative; he demanded the restitution of New France from Britain, but the Kirkes were slow to respond. They were becoming extremely wealthy from their fur trading and did not want to give it up. Samuel Champlain now found himself short of money, and he sold two houses he owned in Brouage.[1] Matters dragged on. He busied himself with his maps and notes, and working toward the publication of *The Voyages to Western New France, called Canada Made by Sieur de Champlain of Saintonge, Captain for the King in the Western Navy, with all discoveries he has made in that country from the year 1603 until the year 1629.*[2] The title *sieur* may have been added in a later edition.

With the Kirkes still strongly in control of Quebec, Richelieu and the Company of Hundred decided to give aid to the place in Acadia that still had a French presence — the little settlement around Charles de La Tour's trading post, then on mainland Cape Sable. The company sent two supply ships carrying settlers and two Franciscan priests to Cape Sable. La Tour would appreciate the reinforcements.[3]

In July 1631, King Charles ordered the Kirkes to return Quebec, but slowness of communication would keep them there for a while. Champlain began asking for Acadia to be returned at the same time. To add to his frustrations over delays, his marriage was in trouble. Hélène had decided she wanted to live a religious life. She had become friendly with some Ursuline nuns and she wanted to join the order and move to their convent. He asked her not to leave, at least not until the future of New France could be decided. He knew a separation would be regarded as a divorce, and wanted to avoid a scandal that would make him a non-person to King Louis and his courtiers. In February 1632, the couple divided their properties, and separated while remaining in the same house.[4]

> ## FASCINATING FACT
> ### Quebec and Acadia Returned to France
>
> Reluctantly, Viceroy Richelieu agreed to send Champlain as governor of Quebec, while Samuel's good friend, Isaac de Razilly, would govern Acadia.

Some evidence, interpreted by more contemporary Canadian historians, suggests that Champlain made a voyage to Cape Breton in 1632. It was not mentioned by any earlier writers nor in his major works, but such a journey would be in character for the much-travelled hero. Marcel Trudel and Lucien Campeau both decided that the obscure record revealed the truth.[5] The reason for the voyage was to visit Fort Anne, in a sheltered spot on the shore of the island west of the Cabot Strait, to investigate that post.

It must have been a very short visit, as other developments were crowding in. On March 29, 1632, the Treaty of Saint-Germain-en-Laye was signed, restoring Quebec and Acadia to France and ordering Scotland to evacuate Acadia.[6]

Richelieu offered a commission to Isaac de Razilly as the cardinal/viceroy's lieutenant at Quebec. Razilly returned the document unsigned. He allegedly told the viceroy he would prefer to serve under Champlain, who was better qualified.[7]

Now that the treaty had been signed, when he offered Acadia to Razilly, the naval officer gladly accepted and hastily got an expedition ready. Champlain, still with high hopes for the maritime colony, thought his dear friend an excellent choice.

The cardinal bypassed Champlain by appointing Émery de Caën to enter Quebec and remove the British. The two de Caëns had spent the past three years continuing to trade in the St. Lawrence River Valley and sailing regularly for France. They found many secluded coves and streams along the great river where their ship, like many foreign ones, could be safely hidden.[8] Richelieu of course selected Catholic Émery over Protestant Guillaume.

In September 1632, Razilly arrived in Acadia with three sailing vessels, 300 hand-picked men, three Capuchin fathers, and a few women and children. One man who was to play an important part in the future of Acadia was the nobleman Charles de Menou d'Aulnay, a cousin of Razilly. Both men were from Tours as were many of the new arrivals. D'Aulnay was the captain of the armed ship sent to convoy the other vessels, which were loaded with people and supplies. He was also ruthless toward anyone who stood in his way.[9]

Razilly chose a site at the mouth of La Haye River for his settlement. The workers constructed Fort Sainte Marie de Grace to protect the colony (which he named La Have, after its river). It was halfway between two fishing posts: Cape Sable and Canso.[10]

Back in Paris, Richelieu was looking for a suitable man as his lieutenant for the St. Lawrence River Valley. On March 1, he grudgingly awarded the job to the bourgeois Samuel Champlain. On March 23, aided by the One Hundred Associates, he was at Dieppe with three small, heavily loaded ships, the *Saint-Pierre*, *Don de Dieu*, *and Saint-Jean*, with 150 colonists, some new Jesuit priests, the crew, and enough materials to restore what Champlain feared would be a Quebec in near ruins.[11] As was customary, a priest conducted the farewell ceremony, the blessing of the boats.

The crossing started off smoothly, Champlain was navigator, but they fought weather and then fog that scattered his ships. They called at Tadoussac, finding English ships with whom they could trade, and reached Quebec on May 22, receiving a hero's welcome — a salute from the guns at the old habitation. Everyone had turned out: habitants; Jesuits who had arrived in 1632, led by Father Paul Le Jeune, the superior in Canada; and Montagnais, who arrived from their surrounding villages and camps. There were no Récollets; the One Hundred Associates had decided not to permit men of the poorer order to come back.[12]

The first task for his workers was a place of worship where Champlain could thank his maker for the happiness of being where he belonged again. He named it Notre Dame de la Recouvrance.[13]

No more was recorded of the three adopted Montagnais daughters. And there was much speculation about Étienne Brûlé. When the people of Quebec learned that their great leader was coming home, the one-time interpreter vanished. The popular opinion was that he went to Huronia, where he had been happy among the Bear Clan, who were his particular friends. The Huron, worried that Champlain might disapprove if they befriended him, turned against him. After torturing him they killed and cannibalized him![14] Much discussion revealed unproven details; the only thing that is factual is that the Huron, probably of the Bear Clan, murdered Etienne Brûlé.

Neither grave nor bones have been identified. What is most sad is that Brùlé is best remembered as a traitor. He deserved to be known as among the earliest and foremost European explorers of the Great Lakes basin and its surroundings. By the western shore of the sprawling city of Toronto, at the mouth of the Humber River, is Brûlé Park. There stands a historical plaque in honour of the first Frenchman who, accompanied by Huron guides, canoed down the Humber to Lake Ontario.

In 1968, the Ontario government passed legislation for individual French-language schools for French-speaking Ontarians. In September 1969, doors opened into the École Secondaire Étienne Brûlé, to serve the greater Toronto area. It was one of the first French-language public high schools in Ontario.

19 Peopling Quebec, 1633–1635

How disheartened he must have been as he surveyed his town. Fort St. Louis had been finished by the British, but now it needed restoring. The old habitation was useless and work had to resume at once on the new one. The streets were dirty, piled with refuse, and rough to walk on. Champlain was now 63 years old and he needed the energy of a man of 30. Since 1599, in New Spain and in the service of New France he had crossed the Atlantic 26 times, 28 if that run to Cape Breton in 1632 was included, and that was not the full extent of his voyaging. He had made many coastal explorations on seas and fresh waters. However, for the first time, a fresh breeze was blowing throughout France. The shock of the British Kirkes' occupation had awakened the mother country. The new colonists he brought, and those who would follow, were in response to this increased awareness. Populate or lose New France!

Quebec became again a hive of industry. The famous Héberts were fruitful and multiplying with many new surnames as daughters wed. Champlain was proud of his long friendship with this family, and of his part, and Hélène's, in helping them acquire their farm and stone house.

Another family of note was the Martins, Abraham and his French wife, Marguerite Langlois. Abraham was nicknamed l'Écossais because of his Scottish origin. He had lived in Dieppe around 1619, where he married Marguerite and soon moved on to New France. At first Martin made his living at fishing and sailing a company barque. Their son, Eustache (named after Hélène's brother, perhaps?) who arrived in 1621, has been called the first French baby born in North America. The Martins left Quebec when the Kirkes took it, and returned via Dieppe in 1632.[1]

He and Marguerite had six daughters, who produced many children. If Louis Hébert is the ancestor of French Canadians, they are also descended from Abraham Martin. As well as seafaring, Martin had farmland, some of it granted by Champlain. It was supposed to be on the plains, hence the name the Plains of Abraham. This is a matter of debate, though; some claim the farm was elsewhere, while others argue that the location is correct.

Among the most useful of all was Robert Giffard de Moncel, a wealthy apothecary from Perche, near Normandy, who came to Quebec as surgeon on a ship in 1621 or 1622. He was a humanist and a kindred spirit to Champlain. He wanted to fulfill his hero's plan for a mixed race by marrying a Native woman. She agreed, but her family would not accept him and he left the colony. He returned in 1627 and built a cabin, but he was captured by some of the Kirkes' followers and robbed. He somehow escaped and got home to France, and with Champlain's support he applied to the One Hundred Associates for a grant of land. He received his land on both sides of the Beauport River on the east side of the Rock, and brought out colonists at his own expense.[2]

Champlain welcomed all comers. Richelieu dictated population increase through births among Catholic parents born in New France, rather than by immigration. He did not want any Huguenots slipping past him. Again, the two were at odds. His lieutenant on the scene sent reports to the cardinal, asking for a force of 150 soldiers to keep the peace and guard against invasion, but his viceroy did not reply.[3]

The only French soldiers at Quebec were a small honour guard stationed at Fort St. Louis. Champlain probably did what he had done in 1611 — raising militia companies from among his civilian traders. Those men had accompanied him in the second strike at the Mohawk warriors in their barricade of logs on the site of Sorel, close to the exit of the Richelieu River.

Quebec was growing. A new settlement at Three Rivers was taking shape. By 1634, Champlain was voyaging as far as that settlement, and building fortified trading posts upstream on islands in the St. Lawrence. All the while he sought to maintain alliances with the Montagnais, their Algonquin close relatives, and other friendly nations.

He was making contacts with some of the Iroquois, more acceptable now to his traditional allies because many from both factions wanted an end to the warfare. So far, the Mohawk warriors had concentrated their strength against other Aboriginal nations. They had been quiet since the drubbing of 1610, nearly three decades earlier. Champlain was the expert at talking and at easing tensions. As long as he was in charge, things remained relatively calm and sharp exchanges were rare.

The new settlers were taking up land on the first seigneuries, where a new system of land division was popular. Since waterways were the best means of travel, the farm lots were laid out in *rangs*, or "ranges," in long narrow strips, still evident in the rural landscapes along the St. Lawrence River Valley in the twenty-first century. The ranges had two advantages; each farm would have a piece of water frontage, for communication, for trips to the parish church, and the larger centres. They also gave dwellers close proximity to neighbours and families, and acted as street-villages. When, in the 1740s, French settlers took up land along both sides of the Detroit River, maps show the same settlement pattern of strips with access to the water.[4]

The Jesuits were busy expanding their missions and planning an elementary school for Huron boys. By 1635, they had opened their *College des Jesuits*.[5] Since it was not in Huronia, but in Quebec, by implication it was a boarding school — the first residential school for Aboriginal children, now regarded as a terribly misguided notion that caused a great deal of harm to the Native peoples. The idea was the same, to turn the boys into French-speaking Catholic farmers of the Algonquin nations of the forest or the Huron with their traditional form of farming and culture.

With the coming of spring, Samuel Champlain worked less energetically than he had in the past. He was slowing down, showing signs of weakness as the days passed. As autumn arrived he was nearly bedridden. In October he suffered a massive stroke that left him paralyzed. He delegated some of his duties to a trusted friend, François Derré de Gand, a member of the One Hundred Associates.[6] Among other friends who kept vigils at his bedside were Héberts, Couillards, Martins, Giffards, a Montagnais godson, Father Le Jeune, and his Jesuit followers.

On November 17, he prepared his will, aided by friends and servants. It was a very long document, with many bequests to individuals and religious institutions. The sum of 600 livres was to be paid to Marguerite, one of the daughers of Abraham and Marguerite Martin, if she married a man who lived in New France: otherwise, she would not receive her inheritance. There were other similar amounts to encourage young people to stay and aid in the peopling. To his wife Hélène he left a wax medallion of the Lamb of God, a gold ring with a stone, and a bundle of her favourite grey fox furs. She did not need his financial support; she had a large inheritance from her own family.

The remainder, not specified, was for the Holy Virgin Mother, through the expansion and improvement of his chapel, Notre Dame de la Recouvrance. He wanted it to become a great church or cathedral.[7]

Around the same time as he was preparing his will, his treasured friend and lieutenant-general of Acadia, Isaac de Razilly, died unexpectedly at La Have (now La Héve). Razilly had done an excellent job of rebuilding his colony, in co-operation with Charles de Menou d'Aulnay at Port Royal and Charles de Saint-Étienne de La Tour at Cape Sable. Unlike Samuel Champlain, Razilly had received strong support from their viceroy and his relative, Cardinal Richelieu.[8]

It is uncertain whether Champlain knew of Razilly's death. Near Christmas his own time was close. Quebec was a joyous place on Christmas Eve, as the whole town and its surroundings were in high spirits. At Fort St. Louis, the guard fired a cannon to mark the birth of Christ and followed with a *feu de joie* ("fire of joy" — a celebratory bonfire). Midnight Mass was in his chapel and crowds grew as the whole populace celebrated the holy birth. By daylight, with Father Charles Lalemant praying, Fathar Le Jeune recorded:

> On the twenty-fifth of December, the day of the birth of our Saviour upon earth, Monsieur de Champlain, our Governor was reborn in heaven. The least we were able to say is that his death was full of blessings.[9]

Samuel Champlain was dead. Father Paul Le Jeune conducted the funeral oration in a crowded Notre Dame de la Recouvrance. Outside waited, again, almost the entire population, who were mourning in the streets and walking in a procession. The Jesuits were in their black robes, soldiers in white and blue with gold helmets and breastplates, well-dressed seigneurs,

Archives of Ontario, F1152, Container 3, Series B293935.

The Champlain monument in Orillia, Ontario. It was unveiled on July 1, 1925, at Couchiching Beach Park. Standing at over nine metres high, the monument was created in England by artist Vernon March and shipped to Canada.

hundreds of habitants in homemade clothes, and First Nations in their furs. All gathered to mark the passing of the man they well knew had been, more than anyone or group, responsible for the survival of the colony.

No one knows where his remains lie. He was no doubt buried in the chapel he loved, but it burned to the ground five years after his passing. His death was as mysterious as his birth — no records exist. He was born somewhere near Brouage, and laid to rest somewhere near the cathedral that grew in place of his chapel.

Some attempts to give him a picture show nothing of the real man. Fischer suggests a smallish man, as indicated in a sketch he drew of the fight with the Mohawks at Lake Champlain. A statue, unveiled in Quebec City in 1898 stands on the Dufferin Terrace, high above the St. Lawrence. The sculptor was Paul Chère, but it is not a true likeness. Another, unveiled in 1915 on Parliament Hill in Ottawa, is by sculptor Hamilton MacCarthy, who depicted our hero as holding an astrolabe aloft. Fischer writes that he is shown holding it the wrong way up; it would have dangled down from his fingers. A third monument is at Plattsburgh, New York, a sturdy sculpture by Carl Augustus Heber, dated 1912. It is the only one that depicts Champlain as a soldier, with helmet, padded protected waistcoat, and what may be intended to represent a harquebus, the top of the barrel grasped in his left hand.[10]

One lingering task remained for Cardinal Richelieu. In January 1636, before word of Samuel Champlain's death had reached France, the viceroy had replaced him. The new man was a noble, of course, and of considerable prestige, a Knight of Malta, named Charles Huault de Montmagny, the first appointed governor of Quebec. Instead of depending on his lieutenant, Montmagny would be the first governor to take up residence in the colony. The population, owing largely to Champlain's persistence since 1633, had risen eightfold, from scarcely 50 to a respectable 400 people.[11]

20 Aftermath, 1636–1650

Charles Huault de Montmagny was no Samuel Champlain. He was the sort of Catholic nobleman Cardinal Richelieu favoured. He governed for 12 years, until 1648. He seemed like a conservative man who believed in the protection of his subjects from threats by the Iroquois Confederacy. He built a stone fort and began new walls around Quebec City, plus a new wooden fort and stockade for Three Rivers. A second new wooden fort stood at the entrance to the Richelieu River, the site of Sorel, to guard against incursions by Iroquois war parties. He made a few attempts at peacemaking, but never achieved Champlain's great successes.[1]

Two years after Champlain's death, a judge ruled his will to the Virgin Mary invalid, and settled in favour of Marie Camaret, a cousin of the Champlain family.[2] Two more years later, the Jesuits opened a training centre for First Nations peoples at Sillery. It was an attempt to turn them into French-speaking Catholic farmers. In 1638, the wealthy Madame de la Peltrie founded a school for Aboriginal girls in Quebec.[3] Both had limited success.

There is an old saying: "You can take the boy out of the country, but you can't

FASCINATING FACT
What Became of Châtelaine Hélène?

Ten years after his passing , in 1645, Hélène chose life as an Ursuline nun. She founded a new convent of the Ursulines at de Meaux, France, where she died in 1654.

take the country out of the boy." Amended, it might say, "You can take the child out of the forest but you can't take the forest out of the child." A few, especially girls, became sincere converts, but many more only pretended to adopt the colonial religion, or ran away over the palisade. Algonquin preferred small bark shelters to cold walls of a French house or convent, and Huron felt more at ease in their sociable longhouses. Most of the pupils in both schools were from French families.

The year 1639 saw the arrival of Marie de l'Incarnation, with two Ursulines to establish a convent, while two Augustine nursing sisters arrived to open Hôtel-Dieu, the first hospital.[4]

Marie de l'Incarnation.

A Civil War in Acadia

The death of Isaac de Razilly in 1635 had deadly serious consequences for Acadia. His brother, Claude, was appointed to succeed him, but as he did not want to cross the Atlantic, he made Isaac's lieutenant, Charles de Menou d'Aulnay, the resident governor. Meanwhile, Charles de Saint-Étienne de La Tour, who had defended Cape Sable during the Kirkes' attacks, was visiting France. He was received by Louis XIII, who rewarded him for keeping his part of Acadia free by appointing him governor of the colony. This led to trouble between La Tour and the warlike d'Aulnay.

Dessin de Aristide Beaugrand-Champagne

LE PREMIER HÔPITAL DE VILLE-MARIE OU MAISON DE MLLE MANCE, 1645, BERCEAU DE L'HÔTEL-DIEU ACTUEL

Sur la seconde façade se profile le petit oratoire; à l'arrière plan, à droite, l'historique fossé où se cachaient les Sauvages
(Emplacement de la rue St-Dizier)

Hôtel-Dieu, the first hospital in New France. The modern-day hospital in Montreal is located on the very same site.

Collections des Religieuses Hospitalières de Saint-Joseph.

By 1638, France tried to solve the problem of two governors for the same territory by partition, so that each governor would have his own share. By this time, d'Aulnay was settled at Port Royal, on the Nova Scotia peninsula. La Tour had moved from Cape Sable to the mouth of the Saint John River, where the fur trading was more rewarding, and built Fort La Tour. Far away in France, the king's counsellors had less than a vague notion of the map or shape of Nova Scotia and New Brunswick. They gave La Tour the peninsula, the south side of the Bay of Fundy. To d'Aulnay they gave the territory behind Fort La Tour

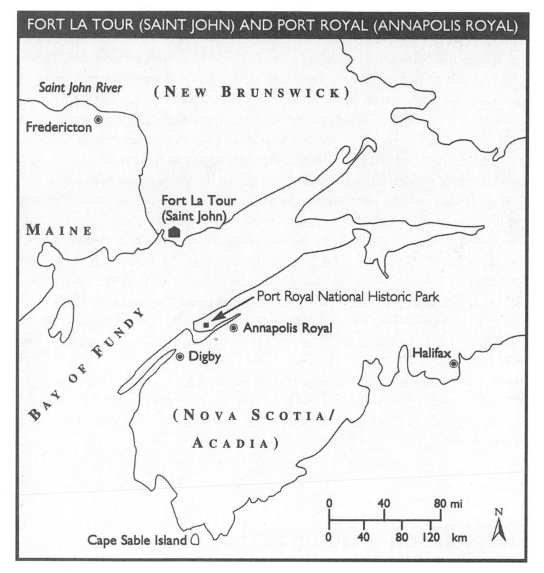

FORT LA TOUR (SAINT JOHN) AND PORT ROYAL (ANNAPOLIS ROYAL)

Saint John River

(NEW BRUNSWICK)

Fredericton

MAINE

Fort La Tour
(Saint John)

Port Royal National Historic Park

⊙ Annapolis Royal

BAY OF FUNDY

⊙ Digby

Halifax

(NOVA SCOTIA/
ACADIA)

0   40   80 mi

0   40   80   120   km

N

Cape Sable Island

Map of Acadia, circa 1635.

— the north side of Fundy. Thus each rival's trading fort was in the other's territory, as shown on map? This arrangement made it necessary for each governor to keep a garrison to guard his base.[5]

Fort La Tour had become a formidable habitation with three cannons facing the harbour and a main bastion of masonry walls nearly a metre thick. Soldiers and supplies arrived from France. D'Aulnay also hired soldiers in France, and so things went until February 1645. La Tour was in Boston purchasing food and trade goods. D'Aulnay, who now had a 16-gun flagship, named the *Grand Cardinal*, attacked Fort La Tour, but was driven away by the sudden return of La Tour. By April, when La Tour was again in Boston, d'Aulnay appeared with a fleet and 200 men off Fort La Tour, where the defenders numbered only 47. In charge, with her baby son in her arms, was Madame de La Tour. She was forced to surrender. To make up for his losses, d'Aulnay then tortured all but two of the prisoners to death, forcing Madame de La tour to watch. Of the two who were spared, one was thought to be the executioner, the other a Swiss mercenary.

After three weeks, Madame de La Tour died because of the horrors she had witnessed. D'Aulnay had her buried and sent her baby to France; nothing more was heard of the child. Then fearing a sudden appearance of La Tour, d'Aulnay packed up and sailed for Port Royal. Meanwhile, La Tour had received word of the fate of his post, but he had failed to raise a force in Boston to retake it. And then La Tour was in Quebec for a while, trading there between 1645 and 1649.

On a day in May 1650, d'Aulnay was drowned when his canoe overturned. He left behind his wife, Jeanne, and four boys and four girls. La Tour paid a visit to sympathize with her. The two married and had three daughters and two sons. La Tour was reinstated as sole governor of Acadia.[6]

——— ——— ———

The Destruction of Huronia, 1649

From 1641 to 1649 there were occasional periods of attack by the Iroquois, followed by periods of peace. In 1648, Governor Montmagny retired. His successor was another French nobleman (even though Richelieu had died in 1642, his rules lived on). The new man was Louis d'Ailleboust de Coulonge et d'Argentenay. He had sailed from France in 1643 to take a leading role in establishing Ville-Marie (Montreal), a new Catholic outpost. As governor, he could not prevent the Iroquois from annihilating nearly the entire Huron nation.[7]

Library and Archives Canada, C-007885, Acc. No. 1936-239-1.

Ville-Marie in 1642.

The Iroquois were much more dangerous in the 1640s, after they had traded their pelts for firearms from the Dutch and the British. By 1649, Huronia was a burned ruin. Some survivors joined the Iroquois. Others, with the few remaining Jesuits, went to Christian Island, in Lake Simcoe, and later they went east to settle around Lorette, north of Quebec City. Still others went to Michigan and became known as *Wendats*, later *Wyandots*. Sainte-Marie Among the Hurons, the large fortified Jesuit mission in the neighbourhood, was closed. Now it has been restored as a centre for remembering these First Nations in the Georgian Bay-Wye River area.

Had Champlain lived longer, would his talent for persuasion have served the people of Huronia any better? Had his successors used too much force, instead of just enough?

The vast stone Martyrs' Shrine in Midland serves as the memorial to the sufferings of eight Jesuits who died; most of them tortured by the Iroquois warriors. They were six priests, Fathers Jean de Brébeuf, Anthony Daniel, Charles Garnier, Isaac Joques, Gabriel Lalemant, and Noël Chabanel, and two lay brothers, René Goupil and Jean de la Lande. Sainthood was conferred on them in 1930.

Sainte-Marie Among the Hurons, an overview. This oblique artist's representation shows the extent of the Jesuit headquarters in Huronia.

Ontario Department of Tourism and Information.

Francophone Populations and Cultures

Author John Ralston Saul sees Canada as founded by three groups: the English (or British), the French, and the Aboriginal. Samuel Champlain founded three Francophone populations: in Quebec, in Acadia, and the Métis. To him the third population would not be distinct, but a new people of shared heritages.

The Indian Act did not serve the Métis people fairly. A man who married a non-Indian woman retained his treaty rights, and family members were Indians. However, where a woman married a non-Indian man, she lost her treaty rights and her children were not Indians. This regulation made sense where a man was expected to take care of his own, but it discriminated against women. As marriage breakdowns became more common, a woman who had lost her treaty rights could not live on her band's reservation. The Indian Act was amended in 1985. Since then treaty rights are not lost; all Indian women and their children have the right to membership in a band. The Act is one of the few places where the term "Indian" is used. Otherwise it's correct to say "First Nations" or "Aboriginals" because "India" was a mistake made by explorer Christopher Columbus when he believed he had discovered India instead of North America!

Historian David H. Fischer recalled that the 1970 Census of Canada showed that some 300,000 people called themselves Métis. Many others could have made the claim, although many may not suspect they are of mixed ancestry. There are Métis Associations in all Canadian provinces, a testimony to the rising numbers of people who know their origins.[8]

——— ——— ———

Who Was Samuel Champlain, the Founder of New France and Canada?

We still have no proof of who his parents were. We don't know whether Champlain's name had a *de*, or if that was added later. Speculations that he was of royal or at least noble blood have not proven. We are free to choose. Do we

The martyrdom of Brébeuf and Lalement, 1649. Europeans could be equally cruel in executing those they considered guilty of crimes.

prefer a natural child of Henry IV or the case for a bourgeois mariner?

One thing is certain beyond all doubt. If he had not had such a powerful urge to see a French colony survive, and had not tried again each time he suffered a setback, Quebec City would not have had its 400th anniversary celebration in 2008.

French Canadians may be French-speaking, but they are not French men and women. They may love visits to France, but they are North Americans who have their own culture. The same applies to sports. Laval University and the city of Montreal have football teams that play the Canadian game. The Montreal Canadiens hockey team may be adored by the fans, but French surnames are widely spread out among all the players of the NHL.

FASCINATING FACT
Vive le Quebec Libre!

Canada celebrated her hundredth anniversary in 1967. Owing to the efforts of Samuel Champlain to build a strong colony, General Charles de Gaulle (also the president of France at the time) had been able to sail his battleship to Wolfe's Cove.

In Montreal, he shouted his spontaneous (but, in reality, well-rehearsed) call to the separatists: "Vive le Quebec Libre!" Prime Minister Lester Pearson, mild as usual, noted that de Gaulle's cry was "not acceptable," causing De Gaulle to depart on his battleship in a foul mood.

In Ottawa, a grand banquet had been planned, but the miffed de Gaulle deliberately avoided going to the capital. Joined by Governor General Roland Michener and Mrs. Michener, Mr. and Mrs. Pearson partook of what they could manage of the feast.

A French-speaking taxi driver in Montreal deplored de Gaulle's impudence. A Canadian war veteran, he sorrowed over the loss of Canadian lives during the liberation of France from the Nazis. De Gaulle blindly believed that Quebec should separate, making two nations based on mother tongue.

After the Aftermaths: King Louis XIV, Two Legacies

Louis XIV was born in 1638. He became king in 1643 at age five. He had a shorter time of parenting than his father Louis XIII. By 1661, Louis, at the age of 23, was ruling directly, and had taken a special interest in the future of Quebec. He proclaimed the colony a royal province, eligible for public funds. With the population still only a mere 2,500, it might fall easy prey to France's European rivals. The new funds permitted much more rapid growth, although it never caught up to its neighbours.

Louis XIV's other act was less admirable. By 1685, now 47, he decided to punish the Huguenots for not being Catholics. He revoked the Edict of Nantes that had permitted the civil and religious rights of Protestants. The consequence is a legitimate part of Champlain's story because the religious conflicts had been with him all his life. From his soldiering on behalf of the Huguenots through his conversion and strong Catholic faith, he retained his tolerance. For a man of his convictions, Louis XIV's action was a disaster as Huguenots were the business class. Over the next few years, 400,000 Huguenots left France, some going to the German states, to Holland, England, the Thirteen Colonies of North America, and to South Africa, where in 1688 they settled in and around the town of Paarl. They introduced the art of growing vines and making of fine wines.

At Franschhoek, the heart of the wine country, stands a lofty, dignified monument to the Huguenots. Their descendants make up about one fifth of the Afrikaans-speaking population.

Photo by Geoff Fryer.

The Huguenot Monument in Franschhoek, South Africa, is dedicated to the cultural influences brought about by the Huguenot immigration to the Cape Colony during the seventeenth and eighteenth centuries. The monument was designed by J.C. Jongens and unveiled by Dr. A.J van der Merwe on April 17, 1948.

Appendix A

Champlain's Publications

(1601) *Brief Narrative of the Most Remarkable Things that Samuel Champlain of Brouage Observed in the West Indies.*

(1603) *Of Savages, or Voyage of Samuel Champlain of Brouage Made to New France in the Year 1603.*

(1613) *The Voyages of the Sieur de Champlain of Saintonge, Captain in Ordinary for the King in the Navy.* (Covers the years 1604 to 1612)

(1619) *Voyages and Discoveries Made in New France, from the Year 1615 to the End of the Year 1618, by the Sieur de Champlain, Captain in Ordinary for the King in the Western Ocean.*

(1632) *The Voyages to Western New France, called Canada, made by the Sieur de Champlain of Saintonge, Captain for the King in the Western Navy, with all discoveries he has made in that country from the year 1603 until the year 1629.*

(1632) *A Treatise on Maritime Affairs, and the Duty of a Good Mariner. Published with Voyages to Western New France etc.* and included by H.P. Biggar in his edition of *the Works of Champlain*, CWB, to 1922–1936, as Vol. 6, 253–346.

(1922–1936) *The Works of Samuel de Champlain.* The Champlain Society, H.P. Biggar, ed. (CWB) Toronto.

Appendix B

Chronology

1570
Probable birth of Champlain, only child of Antoine and Marie Le Roy; no record of birth or baptism.
Wars of religion begin in France.

1576
Ships fish in Gulf of St. Lawrence.
Catholic League is formed to suppress Protestantism.

1593
Champlain enlists in army of Henri IV, as billet master.
Henri IV converts to Catholicism and is crowned in Chartres.

1598
Champlain receives pension from the king.

Henri IV proclaims the Edict of Nantes that allowed Protestants civil rights.
Champlain joins his uncle, Guillaume Halléne (or Hellaine) for voyage to Cadiz.
Voyages de Jacques Cartier is published.

1599
First Atlantic crossing for Champlain; start of two years visiting New Spain.

1600
French start a trading post at Tadoussac, de Mons and Pont-Gravé present.
Henri IV weds Marie de' Medici of Tuscany.

1601
Publication of *Brief Narrative of the Most Remarkable Things that Samuel Champlain of Brouage Observed in the West Indies*.
Future King Louis XIII is born.
Death of uncle, Guillaume Hellaine, who willed a large estate near La Rochelle to Champlain.

1603
Aymar de Chaste trading expedition, led by Pont-Gravé and de Mons, with Champlain as observer, to explore upper St. Lawrence.
Publication of *Of Savages, or Voyage of Samuel Champlain of Brouage Made to New France in the Year 1603*.
Death of de Chaste.

1604
De Mons succeeds de Chaste, sails for Acadia with Champlain as geographer, and Poutrincourt with settlers for Port Royal.
"Habitation" at St. Croix, island in St. Croix River.
Champlain explores part of Atlantic coast. Severe winter follows.

Chronology

1605

Of 79 men at St. Croix, 35 die of scurvy. Colony is moved to Port Royal.

1606

Poutrincourt starts seigneury at Port Royal, crops are planted, and water mill, brick oven, pine tar oven for caulking ships are constructed.

Marc Lescarbot, writer, creates first play for North America, *The Neptune Theatre*.

Champlain invents the Order of Good Cheer, to ease boredom of long winters.

1607

King Henri revokes de Mons's trade monopoly, Champlain returns to France having mapped the coast from Cape Breton to Cape Blank (Cape Cod).

Jamestown, Virginia, first English settlement is founded.

Scottish settlers arrive in Acadia and name it Nova Scotia.

1608

De Mons is granted new trade monopoly. Champlain, as his lieutenant, founds Quebec, builds the habitation, quells plot to have him assassinated, ringleader executed.

Threat from Basque fishermen and traders.

First winter at Quebec a disaster, resulting in cases of scurvy and dysentery.

1609

Publication of Marc Lescarbot's *History of New France*.

Champlain forms alliance with the Huron and some Algonquin nations.

First battle with the Iroquois and defeat of Mohawk warriors on Lake Champlain.

English explorer Henry Hudson, in pay of the Dutch, sails from Manhattan north to the site of Albany, a new threat to Quebec.

1610

Second defeat of the Mohawk warriors.

Champlain, now about 40 years old, returns to France, marries 12-year-old Hélène Boullé, daughter of the king's minister of finance.

Assassination of Henri IV, succeeded by nine-year-old Louis XIII, with mother, Marie de' Medici, as regent.

1611

Back in Quebec, Champlain goes to Sault St. Louis (Lachine Rapids) and establishes a trading post. He named the island of Saint Helen's after his wife.

France and Spain form an alliance through the Treaty of Fontainebleau.

Henry Hudson's sailors mutiny and abandon him to die.

1612

Champlain becomes Lieutenant of New France; is governor under viceroys Soissons, then Condé.

1613

Champlain travels up the Ottawa River and is the first European to describe it.

English settlers destroy French property at Port Royal.

Publication of *The Voyages of the Sieur de Champlain of Saintonge, Captain in Ordinary for the King in the Navy* for the period 1604–1612, and map of New France.

1614

Champlain forms Company of Merchants of Rouen and St. Malo and gains monopoly of fur trade.

1615

Champlain brings first four Récollet priests to New France.

Louis XIII, aged 14, weds the Infanta, Anne of Austria.

1616

First French woman lands in Quebec, dies soon after.

The Duke of Richelieu becomes secretary of state for War and Foreign Affairs.

Jesuit Pierre Biard, who went to Acadia in 1611, publishes his *Relation of New France*.

1617

After arrest of Condé, Champlain is briefly unemployed, then becomes lieutenant to new viceroy, the Marquis of Thémines.

Louis XIII governs personally at age 16.

Louis Hébert and his wife and three children become first family to settle in Quebec.

A Dutch trading post is founded on Manhattan.

1618

Champlain's two briefs advocate the establishment of a trading colony on St. Lawrence, made up of at least 15 Récollets, 300 families, and 300 soldiers.

Start of Thirty Years' War to restore Catholic religious unity after Lutheran schism.

1619

Publication of *Voyages and Discoveries Made in New France, from the Year 1615 to the End of the Year 1618, by the Sieur de Champlain, Captain in Ordinary for the King in the Western Ocean.*

First black slaves in North America arrive in Jamestown.

1620

Champlain arrives in New France with his wife Hélène; they stay four years.

He begins construction of Fort St. Louis, on Cape Diamond.

Formation of fur trade Company de Caën.

Arrival of the fabled *Mayflower* with Puritan settlers at Plymouth, Massachusetts.

1621

Hébert's daughter, Guillemette, weds Guillaume Couillard.

Construction of Récollet convent in Quebec.

King James I (of England and VI of Scotland) grants Scotsman William Alexander the right to create a trading company in Nova Scotia/Acadia.

1624

Samuel and Hélène return to France. She never returns to New France.

Richelieu, now a cardinal, becomes first minister of France.

In New Netherlands, the Dutch found a village named New Amsterdam.

1625

The first Jesuits arrive in Quebec, among them Fathers Charles Lalemant and Jean de Brébeuf.

In England, Charles I becomes king.

1626

Champlain returns to Quebec with more Jesuits and some 20 skilled workmen. He has a farm at Cap Tourmente developed for raising cattle.

Isaac de Razilly's brief to Richelieu recommending speedy populating of New France by founding a large trading company in order to catch up with the English and Dutch.

The Dutch buy the island of Manhattan from the Aboriginals for about 24 dollars worth in artificial jewels.

1627

Richelieu becomes Viceroy of New France, forms the Company of One Hundred Associates, holds a monopoly of the fur trade, and becomes responsible for populating colony and converting the First Nations peoples. Charter advocates all-Catholic population and bans Protestants.

In France, British troops arrive to aid Huguenots of La Rochelle, but are defeated at nearby Island of Ré.

Death of Louis Hébert. Widow Marie marries M. Rollet.

In England, the Company of Adventurers is raised to drive French from North America.

1628

Champlain adopts three Montagnais girls: Foi, Espérance, and Charité.

In England, the notorious privateer Kirke brothers set out to intercept ships of the One Hundred Associates and take over Acadia and Quebec.

By order of Richelieu, the One Hundred Associates send four unarmed ships bearing 400 Norman settlers and provisions.

The ships are attacked by the Kirkes and are captured except for small ones who return to France. The Kirkes pillage habitations at Tadoussac, Tourment, and establish a post at Miscou Island.

Champlain refuses to surrender Quebec. The Kirkes return to England with booty.

1629

The Kirkes return and seize Quebec and most of Acadia. Champlain surrenders and is taken to Tadoussac as prisoner. His three adopted daughters are sent home or to Marie Rollet, widow of Louis Hébert.

Peace of Susa ends the Anglo-French war and orders return of all conquests.

Champlain learns that the peace treaty was signed six months before the Kirkes took Quebec, therefore making this an illegal act of war.

1630

The Kirkes rule over the St. Lawrence and take over the fur trade.

Louis XIII exiles the Queen Mother.

London ignores French demands for return of all of New France.

The One Hundred Associates send supply ships to Cape Sable, bringing new settlers and two Franciscan priests.

1632

Jesuits gain a monopoly on all Canadian missions.

The Treaty of Saint-Germain-en-Laye sees all of New France returned to France.

Richelieu sends Isaac de Razilly to Acadia as governor; has the British surrender to Émery de Caën.

1633

Richelieu relents, Champlain is again appointed lieutenant to govern Quebec.

He arrives with three ships, 200 settlers and workers, building materials, supplies, has a chapel built, Notre Dame de la Recouvrance.

1635

Champlain suffers severe stroke and paralysis and dies on Christmas Day. His will leaves most of his possessions to the Virgin Mary, but is overturned in favour of a cousin.

In Quebec, Jesuits open a college for boys, intended for young Huron.

1636

In January, before news of Champlain's death reaches France, Richelieu has replaced him with Charles Huault de Montmagny, first actual governor of the colony, population about 400.

1641

Iroquois declare war on the French.

1642

Cardinal Richelieu dies.

1643

First Iroquois attack on Ville-Marie (Montreal).

Louis XIV becomes king at age five.

1649

Martyrdom of Brébeuf, Lalemant, others. Destruction of Huronia by 1650.

1654

Death of Hélène Boullé, Ursuline nun since 1645.

Notes

Introduction

1. DCB. Trudel, Marcel. *Samuel de Champlain*, Vol. 1, 186–199.

Chapter 1 — Who Was He?
1. Marcel Trudel, *Histoire de la Nouvelle France*, Vol. 1, 255
2. *Encyclopedia Britannica*. "Henry IV of France."
3. David H. Fischer, *Champlain's Dream*, 52.
4. Francine Legaré, *Samuel de Champlain*, 144.
5. H.C. Biggar, CWB. *Champlain, Works of*. From p. 4, Chapter 2, full reference.
6. *Ibid*. Vol. 1, 3.
7. Fischer, 42, from CWB, *Voyages, 1632*. Vol. 3, 314–15.

Chapter 2 — Voyaging for the King, 1598–1603
1. Fischer, 78–79, Chronology, 574.
2. *Encylopedia Britannica*, "Sir Francis Drake."
3. Fischer, 78–83, from Biggar, CWB.
4. *Ibid*. "Chronology of Champlain's Voyages", 574; Legaré, Chronology, 1598, 144–45.

5. Biggar, CWB, Vol. 1, 43; Vol. 1, 46.

6. Fischer, 99–100; Legaré, Chronology, 1601, 145.

7. Fischer, 99, from CWB, Vol. 1, 68.

8. Legaré, Chronology, 1601, 145.

9. Trudel, *DCB*, Vol. 1, 186; Legaré, Chronology, 1601, 145.

10. Fischer, Chapter 6, 105–111, "Geographer in the Louvre."

11. *Ibid.*, 116–17 and 601, Appendix G, Champlain's Superiors; Legaré, Chronology, 1603145–46.

Chapter 3 — The Tabagie, 1603

1. Colby, *Founder of*, 56 fn.

2. Fischer, Appendix M, 622, mid-sized ships of 100 to 350 tons.

3. Legaré, Chapter 3, 32–36.

4. Fischer, 127, from CWB, Vol. 3, 316.

5. Legaré, Champlain map, 26; Trudel, *Histoire*, Vol. 1 (Montreal, 1963), 260–61.

6. Fischer refers to Alain Beaulieu, "The Birth of the Franco-American Alliance" in R. Litien and D. Vaugenois, eds. *The Birth of French America*. Montreal, 2004, 160.

7. Some time would pass before Champlain could arrange for missionaries, but he would have been thinking about them much earlier.

8. Rayburn, Alan, *Dictionary*, M, Falls of Montmorency.

9. Samuel Eliot Morison, *Samuel de Champlain: Father of New France*. New York, 1972, 32.

10. Fischer, 601–02, Appendix G, Chaplain's Superiors.

11. Legaré, Chronology, 1603, 146.

Chapter 4 — St. Croix, 1604

1. *Encyclopedia Britannica*, Vol. 1, "Barents."

2. Rayburn, *Dictionary*, "Frobisher Bay," 137; Iqaluit, 187.

3. *Ibid.* 137.

4. Biggar, CWB, *Works of Champlain*, Vol. 1, 271.

5. Ross and Deveau, *The Acadians*, 8
6. *Ibid.*, 9.
7. Biggar, CWB, Vol. 1, 271.
8. *Webster's Dictionary*; Fischer, Appendix L, 616–17.
9. Fischer, see for full sketch, 169; Legaré, 38.
10. Ross and Deveau, *Acadians*, 10; Biggar, CWB, Vol. 1, 258–59.
11. Legaré, 44.

Chapter 5 — Port Royal: The First Season, Autumn 1605–Spring 1606
1. Biggar, CWB, Vol. 1, 267, 269–70, 370.
2. Legaré, Chronology, 148.
3. Biggar, CWB, Vol. 1, 351.
4. *Ibid.* Vol. 1, 354–55; Lescarbot, *History of New France*, Vol. 2, 277–78.
5. *Ibid.* Vol. 2, 344, 484–86; Fischer, 206–07, re: Lescarbot and Poutrincourt.

Chapter 6 — Port Royal: The Golden Year, 1606–1607
1. Mary Beacock Fryer, *More Battlefields of Canada*, 14; Ross and Deveau, *Acadians*, 13
2. Legaré, Chronology, 1606, 147.
3. Lescarbot, *History*, Vol. 1, 7–14; Vol. 3, 309.
4. Fischer, 192–200; Lescarbot, *History*, Vol.2, 277 and 253.
5. Charles Colby, *Chronicles*, 52–54.
6. Ross and Deveau, *Acadians*, 11–12.
7. *Ibid.*, 12.
8. Legaré, Chronology, 1610, 149.
9. Ross and Deveau, *Acadians*, 13.
10. *Ibid.*, 14; *Encyclopedia Britannica*, Vol. 1, on Argall.
11. Ross and Deveau, *Acadians*, 15, from M.A MacDonald, *Fortune and La Tour*. Letter from Alphonse Deveau, *Notre héritage acadien*, 55–56.
12. Ross and Deveau, *Acadians*, 14–15.

13. *Ibid.*, 16.

Chapter 7 — Paris to Quebec, 1607–1609

1. Lescarbot, *History*, 1907, Vol. 2, 366–367.
2. Fischer, Appendix G. Champlain's Superiors, 601–02.
3. *Ibid.* Copy of map on 229.
4. Cranston, *Étienne Brûlé*. Foreword, ix.
5. Rayburn, *Dictionary of Canadian Place Names.*
6. Fischer, 241, from CWB, Vol. 2, 12–14.
7. Colby, *Founder of*, quotation, 59.
8. Cranston, *Étienne Brûlé*, 14.
9. Colby, *Founder of*, quotation, 65.
10. *Ibid.*, 66.
11. *Ibid.*, 67–68
12. Fischer, 255, from CWB, Vol. 2, 64.

Chapter 8 — Champlain's Harquebus (Arquebus)

1. *Webster's Dictionary*, "Harquebus."
2. B. Graymont, *The Iroquois etc.*, 55–58.
3. Location is based on author's many visits to the spot.
4. *Encyclopedia Britannica*, articles on musket and harquebus.
5. Lescarbot, *History*, Vol. 3, 231.
6. *Ibid.*
7. Fischer, 273, from CWB (Biggar), Vol. 2, 105.
8. Fischer, Chronology, 577, 1609, dates of sailing and arrival at Honfleur.
9. *Ibid.* from CWB, Vol. 2, 109–110.
10. *Ibid.*, 109.
11. *Ibid.*, 112.

Chapter 9 — Second Battle with the Iroquois, 1610

1. Fischer, Chronology, 577, 1610.
2. *Ibid.*
3. G. Lanctôt, *History*, 107.
4. Fischer, 276, from CWB, Vol. 2, 121.
5. G. Lanctôt, *History*, Vol. 1, 106.
6. Fischer, 278, from CWB, Vol.2, 131–34.
7. Trudel, *Histoire*, Vol. 2, 164, 171.
8. *Ibid.*

Chapter 10 — Bad News, 1610

1. Cranston, *Brûlé*, 30–33.
2. Trudel, *Histoire*, Vol. 2, 1604–1627; Biggar, CWB, Vol. 4, 34.
3. Fischer, Chronology, 578, 1610–1611.
4. *Ibid.*, from Jean Liebel, *Pierre de Mons, sieur de Mons*, 37.
5. Biggar, CWB, Vol. 2, 15; Lescarbot, *History*, Vol. 1, 11; col. 2, 315.
6. Legaré, Chronology, 149, 1610.
7. Fischer, 287, from Robert Le Blant, *La famille Boullé*.
8. Pierre Berton, *My Country*, 1976, 65.
9. Fischer, Chronology, 578, 1611; Cranston, *Brûlé*, 34–35.
10. *Ibid.*
11. *Ibid.*, 36.

Chapter 11 — Closer Contact with France, 1611–1615

1. Biggar, CWB, Vol. 2, 214.
2. Fischer, Chronology, 578, entry for 1612.
3. G. Lanctôt, *History*, 107.
4. *Ibid.*, 106.
5. Legaré, Chronology, 150, entry for 1613.

6. Fischer, 309, photo.
7. *Ibid*. Chronology, 579.
8. *Ibid*., 748, from Le Blant, R., *La famille Boullé*, 55–69.
9. *Ibid*., from Robert Le Blant and René Baudry, *Nouveaux documents sur Champlain et son époque*, Vol. 1, (1560–1622), Ottawa, 1967.
10. Le Blant, R., *Le testament de Champlain*, copy in NAC, Ottawa, 1967.
11. Fischer, Chronology, 579–80, 1615.
12. *Ibid*., 1614.
13. T.G. Marquis, *The Jesuit Missions*, Vol. 54, Chron/Can.

Chapter 12 — Visit to Huronia and Lake Onondaga, 1615–1616

1. Fischer, 323, from CWB, Vol. 3, 332, 35.
2. *Ibid*., 324, from CWB, Vol. 3, 34.
3. MBF. Observations in the area, visits to restored Sainte-Marie Among the Hurons.
4. T.G. Marquis, *The Jesuit Missions*, map, 2.
5. Fischer, Chronology, 580, 1615–1616.
6. MBF, familiar with this route after many visits.
7. Cranston, *Brûlé*, 75–77.
8. *Ibid*., 77 is from CWB.
9. *Ibid*., 79–80.
10. *Ibid*., 80.
11. Legaré, Chronology, 1615, 1151.

Chapter 13 — 1616–1620: Years of Continuing Struggle

1. Fischer, Appendix G, Champlain's Superiors, 602–03.
2. *Canadian Encyclopedia*, 1006, by Jacques Bernier.
3. Cranston, 86–90, from Friar Gabriel Sagard's *Histoire du Canada ... depuis l'an 1615*. Reprint; Paris, 1936, 4 volumes.
4. Fischer, Chronology, 581, Quebec 1617; *Canadian Encyclopedia*, 1060, Louis Hébert.

5. Fischer, 352–53, from CWB, Vol. 2, 324–25.
6. *Encyclopedia Britannica*, "Richelieu."
7. Legaré, Chronology, 1618, 152; Fischer, 357, Chronology, France, 1617–18, 581.
8. *Ibid.*
9. Fischer, 359–61, from François Maureau. *Les Amerindiens dans le ballet de cour a l'époque de Champlain*.
10. Legaré, 168, English translation.

Chapter 14 — Madame Champlain: First Lady of New France, 1620–1624

1. Biggar, CWB, Vol. 4, 369–70, 71; Trudel, *Histoire*, Vol. 2, 264 (1966).
2. Fischer, 367, cites Trudel as having found record of sale, *Histoire*, 264.
3. *Ibid.*, 368.
4. *Ibid.*
5. *DCB*, Trudel, "Samuel de Champlain," Vol. 1, 194.
6. Legaré, Chronology, 1620, 152.
7. Fischer, 374–75.
8. Legaré, Chronology, 1621, 153.
9. Kerr, *Historical Atlas*, text, 16, map, 19.
10. Cranston, *Brûlé*, Chapter 4, 19–26, the two fights with the Mohawks.

Chapter 15 — Work in France, 1624–1626

1. Marquis, *The Jesuit Missions*, Vol. 4 (1916).
2. *Ibid.*, frontispiece, C.W. Jefferys, colour drawing of Récollets, Jesuits, 1625.
3. Marquis, *The Jesuit Missions*, 11–12.
4. *Ibid.*
5. Fischer, 379, 384, from CWB, Vol. 5, 86, 207.
6. Marquis, 11–13.
7. Ibid., 13.
8. Fischer, 389–90, with references to many works on Richelieu; a concise version is in

Encyclopedia Britannica.
9. Fischer, 389.
10. Marquis, 18.
11. *Ibid.*, 19.
12. Legaré, Chronology, 1626, 153.
13. *Ibid*
14. *Canadian Encyclopedia*, Hébert, 1060.
15. Colby, Vol. 3, 124 (1915).

Chapter 16 — The Richelieu Takeover, 1627–1628
1. Fischer, Appendix H, Trading Companies and Monopolies, 1588–1635, 607, "The Trading Company of New France, 1627–1632."
2. *Ibid.*
3. Legaré, Chronology, 1626, 153.
4. Fischer, Chronology, 583, April 29, 1627.
5. Fischer, 404.
6. *DCB*, Vol. 1, biographies of some of the Kirkes; Fryer, *More Battlefields of Canada*, 9–15.
7. Legaré, Chronology, 1628, 154; Fryer, *More Battlefields of Canada*, 11.
8. Colby, *Founder*, 124–25.
9. Legaré, Chronology, 1628, 154.
10. *Ibid.*; Colby, *Founder*, 124–25.
11. Legaré, Chronology, 1628, 154.
12. Fryer, *More Battlefields of Canada*, "First Capture," 11.

Chapter 17 — New France Lost, 1629
1. Fryer, *More Battlefields of Canada*, 14.
2. Legaré, Chronology, 1629, 155; Fryer, 14.
3. Legaré, Chronology, 1628, 154, and 127–28.
4. Cranston, Chapter 11, "Race Without Sex Inhibitions," 63–66. Based on Récollet

Gabriel Sagard's *The Long Journey to the Huron Country*. Republished by the Champlain Society, 1939.

5. Cranston, 104–05.
6. Fischer, 500, referring to note 16, Lucien Campeau, *Monumente*, 808–09, Quebec, 1967; CWB, Vol. 5, 128; *DCB*, Vol. 1, Marsolet, by André Vachon.
7. Fryer, *More Battlefields*, 14; Fischer, 428–29; Trudel, *Histoire*, Vol. 3, 1, 41, 46, 49.
8. Fischer, Chronology, 1630–33.

Chapter 18 — Stalemate, 1630–1633
1. Fischer, Chronology, 585; *DCB*, Vol. 1, biographies of the Kirkes.
2. Legaré, Chronology, 1632, 156, in English.
3. *Ibid.*, 1630, 155.
4. Fischer, Chronology, 1632, 585; Legaré, 87–89.
5. Fischer, 439, from Trudel, *Histoire*, Vol. 3, 1, 58, 60, 62; Campeau, Lucien, "The Last Voyage of Champlain" from Merçure Français, 1633, 81–01.
6. Fischer, Chronology, 585; Ross and Deveau, 16.
7. Fischer, 441, Chronology, 585, from Trudel, *Histoire*, Vol. 3, 1, 121.
8. DCB, Vol. 1, Trudel, "Émory de Caën."
9. Fryer, *More Battlefields of Canada*, "The Acadian Civil War", 1–8.
10. Ross and Deveau, 16–17.
11. Legaré, recorded 200 colonists, Chronology, 1633, 156; Fischer, Chronology, 1633, 585.
12. Marquis, *Jesuit Missions*, 47.
13. Legaré, Chronology, 156.
14. Cranston, Chapter 20, "Brûlé Killed and Eaten," 113–117

Chapter 19: Peopling Quebec, 1633–1635
1. Fischer, 460; *DCB*, "Abraham Martin *dit* l'Écossais etc." by Henry Best.
2. Fischer, 468–69; R. Cole. Harris, *The Seigneurial System in Early Canada*, 22, 25, 55, 119.
3. Fischer, Chronology, 1633–35 and 1633, 585.

4. Canada Department of Mines and Resources, Surveys and Mapping Branch, Scale 1: 50,000. Detroit River area.

5. Legaré, Chronology, 1635, 156.

6. Fischer, 518, from Trudel, *Histoire*, Vol. 3, 1 122, 141, 147.

7. Robert Le Blant, *Testament de Samuel de Champlain*. Copy in the NAC, Ottawa, 1967.

8. Fischer, 605, death, 1635; *Canadian Encyclopedia*, 1977, John G. Reid; Ross and Deveau, 1636, probably an error.

9. *The Jesuit Relations*, Vol. 9, 206–07.

10. Fischer, photographs, 548–551; Legaré, photograph, 132.

11. *Ibid*. Chronology, 1636, 157.

Chapter 20: Aftermath, 1636–1650

1. *Canadian Encyclopedia*, on Montmagny; *DCB*, Vol. 1, Montmagny by Jean Hamelin.

2. Legaré, Chronology, 1636, 157.

3. *Ibid*., 1638, 157

4. *Ibid*., 1639, 157.

5. Fryer, *More Battlefields of Canada*, 1–8, "The Acadian Civil War", from M.A. MacDonald, *Fortune and La Tour: The Civil War in Acadia*, 177–79.

6. Fryer, *ibid*.; Ross and Deveau, 19.

7. *Canadian Encyclopedia*, "D'Ailleboust," by Allan Greer.

8. Fischer, 511.

9. Bosher, *The Gaullist Attack on Canada, 1967–97*, Chapter 4, 38–49.

Bibliography

Biggar, Henry Percival. *The Works of Samuel de Champlain*. 6 volumes. Toronto, Champlain Society, 1922–1936. Biggar is one of Fischer's principal sources. Some sources, other than from Fischer, are used directly from Biggar.

Bosher, J.F. *The Gaullist Attack on Canada, 1967–1997*. Kingston and Montreal: McGill-Queen's University Press, 2000.

Canadian Encyclopedia, The. See James H. Marsh, editor.

Colby, Charles W. *The Founder of New France: A Chronicle of Champlain*. Chronicles of Canada Series. Toronto, 1915.

Costain, Thomas B. *The White and the Gold: The French Regime in Canada*. New York, 1954. Chapters 6 and 7 are on the Champlain years.

Cranston, J.H., *Étienne Brûlé: Immortal Scoundrel*. Toronto: Ryerson, 1969.

Dictionary of Canadian Biography (DCB). Many persons in this work are in Vol. 1.

Eccles, William. J. *France in America*. Toronto: Fitzhenry and Whiteside, 1972.

Fischer, David Hackett. *Champlain's Dream*. Toronto: Knopf Canada, 2008. The most valuable, 834 pages, illustrations, maps. The chronology of voyages is most useful.

Fryer, Mary Beacock. *Battlefields of Canada*. Toronto: Dundurn, 1986. Champlain's drawing of himself.

_____. *More Battlefields of Canada*. Toronto: Dundurn, 1993. Chapter 1, Acadia; Chapter 2, Quebec.

Grant, W.L. ed. *The History of New France*. By Marc Lescarbot. 3 volumes, Toronto. Champlain Society, 1907–1914.

Graymont, Barbara. *The Iroquois in the American Revolution*. Syracuse, NY: Syracuse University Press, 1972.

Harris, R. Cole. *The Seigneurial System in Early Canada: a Geographical Study*. University of Wisconsin. Madison, WI, 1968.

Kerr, D.G.G. *A Historical Atlas of Canada*. Toronto: Nelson, 1960.

Lanctôt, Gustave. *A History of Canada from its Origins to the Royal Régime*. Toronto, University of Toronto Press, 1963.

Legaré, Francine. *Samuel de Champlain: Father of New France*. Lantzvillle, B.C.: XYZ Publishing. Translation by Jonathan Kaplansky, 2004. Chronology very useful.

Lescarbot, Marc. *History of New France*. Paris 1609, in French and English in the same year. Translated by W.L. Grant and H. C. Biggar, Champlain Society, 3 volumes., 1919.

Marquis, Thomas Guthrie. *The Jesuit Missions*. Toronto: Chronicles of Canada Series, 1916.

Marsh, James H., ed. *The Canadian Encyclopedia, Year 2000*. Toronto: McClelland & Stewart.

Marshall, Joyce, trans. and ed. *Word from New France. The Selected Letters of Marie de l'Incarnation*. Toronto: Oxford University Press, 1967.

Morison, Samuel Eliot. *Samuel de Champlain: Father of New France*. New York, 1972.

Rayburn, Alan. *Dictionary of Canadian Place Names*. Toronto: Oxford University Press, 1997.

Ross, Sally and Alphonse Deveau. *The Acadians of Nova Scotia*. Halifax: Nimbus, 1992.

Trudel, Marcel. *Histoire de la Nouvelle-France*. Montreal: 3 volumes, 1963, 1966, 1979.

Index

Also by
Mary Beacock Fryer

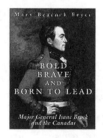

Bold, Brave, and Born to Lead
Major General Isaac Brock and the Canadas
978-1550025019
$12.99

Celebrated as the saviour of Upper Canada, Major-General Sir Isaac Brock was a charismatic leader who won the respect not only of his own troops, but also of the Shawnee chief Tecumseh, and even men among his enemy. His motto could well have been "speak loud and look big." Although this attitude earned him a reputation for brashness, it also enabled his success and propelled him into the significant role he would play in the War of 1812.

Buckskin Pimpernel
The Exploits of Justus Sherwood, Loyalist Spy
978-0919670570
$9.99

At the beginning of the American Revolution, Justus Sherwood left his young family in order to serve with the king's forces, first with General Burgoyne on his disastrous invasion of New York. He was soon appointed Supervisor of Spies and Prisoner Exchanges, and from his "Loyal Blockhouse" on Lake Champlain he sent out raiding parties and spying missions to harass the rebels in New York and England.

What did you think of this book?
Visit www.dundurn.com for reviews, videos, updates, and more!